17.95

DATE DUE

APR 2 0 2001			

DEMCO 38-297

SHIRLEY CHISHOLM

Teacher and Congresswoman

Catherine Scheader

—**Contemporary Women Series**—

ENSLOW PUBLISHERS, INC.

Bloy St. & Ramsey Ave.   P. O. Box 38
Box 777   Aldershot
Hillside, NJ 07205   Hants GU12 6BP
U.S.A.   U.K.

Library of Congress Cataloging-in-Publication Data

Scheader, Catherine.
 Shirley Chisholm, teacher and Congresswoman / by Catherine Scheader.
  p. cm.— (Contemporary women series)
 Includes index.
 ISBN 0-89490-285-7
  1. Chisholm, Shirley, 1924-　—Juvenile literature.
 2. Legislators—United States—Biography—Juvenile literature.
 3. United States. Congress. House—Biography—Juvenile Literature.
 4. Teachers—United States—Biography—Juvenile literature.
 5. Presidential candidates—United States—Biography—Juvenile
 literature. 6. Afro-Americans—Biography—Juvenile literature.
 [1. Chisholm, Shirley, 1924-　. 2. Legislators. 3. Teachers.
 4. Afro-Americans—Biography.] I. Title. II. Series.
 E840.8.C48S34 1990
 328.73'092—dc20
  [B]   89-34451
  [92]   CIP
                                        AC

Printed in the United States of America

10 9 8 7 6 5 4 3 2

Illustration Credits:
American Museum of Natural History, Neg.# 243259, Photo by R.C. Murphy, Courtesy Dept. of Library Services, p. 12; Barbados Board of Tourism, p. 11; Brooklyn Public Library—Brooklyn Collection—Brooklyn Daily Eagle, pp. 18, 25; Courtesy of Shirley Chisholm, pp. 20, 29, 34, 40, 45, 58, 72, 85, 95, 104; Courtesy Gerald R. Ford Library, p. 115; Clemens Kalischer, 1985. Courtesy of Mount Holyoke College, p. 119; National Archives/Nixon Project, p. 88; New York State Department of Economic Development, p. 65; Courtesy of the Franklin D. Roosevelt Library, p. 49; Schomburg Center for Research in Black Culture, The New York Public Library, Astor, Lenox and Tilden Foundations, pp. 54, 109; Courtesy of Spelman College, pp. 6, 122; UPI/Bettmann Newsphotos, p. 77.

Cover Photo: Clemens Kalischer, 1985. Courtesy of Mount Holyoke College.

Acknowledgments

For research assistance, I am indebted to the librarians of the Matawan Public Library, the Alexander Library of Rutgers University, the Brooklyn Public Library and the Schomburg Center for Research in Black Culture, to Jo Moore Stewart of Spelman College, Vee Wailgum of Mount Holyoke College, and Beth Curley of WGBY. Dr. Joseph Ellis, Dr. Richard Moran, and Mrs. Portia Dempsey graciously consented to interviews. To the Honorable Shirley Chisholm, I am most grateful for the time she took to answer my many questions and for her family pictures. Finally, I thank my family and friends and in particular, my husband and favorite reader, Ed.

Contents

Shirley Chisholm, outside the lounge named in her honor at Spelman College.

1

To Barbados and Back

Shirley Anita St. Hill Chisholm was born in Brooklyn in 1924, the first of the four daughters of Charles St. Hill and Ruby Seale St. Hill. Both parents had come from Barbados, an island of the British West Indies. In the early 1920's, they met in Brooklyn, where they lived in a neighborhood of other West Indians, and married.

The small farms of Barbados, like those in the other islands of the Caribbean Sea, could not support all of the population. Only one or two grown children in each family stayed behind in the islands to work on the family farm. Forced to migrate, young people went to the United States, Canada, or England. Those who came to the United States settled in clusters in parts of New York City and the surrounding area.

Ruby Seale was not yet twenty when she and Charles St. Hill were married. The year after Shirley's birth, their second daughter, Odessa, was born, followed two years later by Muriel.

Although many Americans were thriving in the prosperous decade of the 1920's, poor people were struggling. The St. Hills worked hard to support their three young children. Charles's wages as a baker's helper were barely enough to pay the rent and buy food for the family. Ruby sometimes found work as a seamstress, but it was hard to take care of three active children and concentrate on fine sewing too.

Ruby and Charles St. Hill had two dreams that required money. The first was to own a home of their own. The second was to send their children to college.

The St. Hills decided to do what many of their friends from the Islands with the same dreams had already done. They asked Ruby's mother, who still lived in Barbados, to take care of the children. It would not be possible for the whole family to return to the West Indies, because there was no work there. But the children would live with Grandmother Seale for two or three years while Charles and Ruby stayed and worked in Brooklyn. With just the two of them, they could live in a smaller apartment and save money. The savings would give them a head start on their dreams.

While Charles St. Hill kept his job in Brooklyn, Ruby took the girls by ship to Barbados. The trip from Brooklyn to the Caribbean took nine days on a crowded steamer. Even though she was very little at the time, Shirley never forgot it. The sea was rough and they were all sick. When they arrived in the island's capital, Bridgetown, there were more delays. They had to wait on a long, slow-moving line. Customs officers checked everyone's belongings for items that were not allowed into Barbados. The health examination that followed made the children cranky and tearful.

Once on the bus to Vauxhall, the village where Grandmother Seale lived, everyone felt better. Passing brightly colored houses with vegetable gardens out front, the bus scattered chickens and small animals off the road. Mrs. St. Hill told them that Grandmother Seale's house was like the ones that they were passing, and that she kept chickens too.

At the end of the bumpy ride through tiny villages and past farmland, they arrived at Grandmother Seale's. A house with many

8

bedrooms, it was big enough for Shirley and her sisters and for the cousins who arrived later that year.

Ruby stayed for six months while the children adjusted to their new home. By the time she was ready to leave, baby Muriel had learned to walk. Too young to understand why they were parting, the children were lost and lonely when she left. Shirley, knowing she was the oldest, tried to be brave in front of her sisters. But she ended up crying just as hard as they did. They stood together in the road, watching the bus disappear in a cloud of dust. The St. Hill sisters lived on the island of Barbados for seven years, much longer than their parents had planned. The Great Depression had come to America, putting people out of work and wiping out lifetime savings.

While Ruby and Charles struggled in Brooklyn, the children thrived on the Seale farm. They were soon joined by four cousins, the children of Ruby's older sister Violet. She too returned to Brooklyn to help her husband save for the family.

Grandmother Seale's home and heart had room for them all. Aunt Myrtle and Uncle Lincoln, a writer for the Bridgetown newspaper, helped to make up for the absent parents. And with seven children nine years old and younger, there was always company.

In the first days on the farm, Shirley explored Grandmother's house. She ran her hand along the smooth bamboo chairs in the parlor and stared into the fiery depths of the great black, cast-iron kitchen range. The outside toilet in the backyard was a surprise to the children from Brooklyn, and so was the outdoor water supply. They soon forgot about kitchen faucets. Every day, a huge galvanized tank next to the house had to be filled with buckets of water from the well. The children were responsible for filling the tank, which stored water for cooking, drinking, and washing.

Grandmother Seale raised not only chickens, but also ducks,

goats, pigs, lambs, and cows. The children, as they grew older, helped to water and care for the animals.

In the garden grew yams, sweet potatoes, pumpkins, and melons. Twice a week, Grandmother Seale and Aunt Violet went to market with women from nearby farms. They carried vegetables and chickens to sell in the village. Going to market was a special treat for the children. On market days everyone gathered to exchange news and buy food for the coming week. The women walked along the road to town, balancing trays of produce on their heads. Shirley imitated them, holding her shoulders straight and her back erect.

Less than a year after her mother returned alone to Brooklyn, Shirley went to school for the first time. She was just four years old. The school in the village of Vauxhall was a white, wooden, one-room building. In that one room were seven classes with 125 children, ranging in age from four to eleven. Barbados and its neighboring islands were then part of the British Commonwealth. The school followed the English traditions, and classes were called "forms." The day began with 125 voices singing "God Save the King" and "Rule Britannia."

When Shirley and her cousins finished school at four o'clock, they walked home from the village and changed their school clothes. Their job was to care for the animals, keep them out of the road and bring them back to the yard before dinner. The smallest children fed the chickens and ducks and gathered eggs. The older ones carried water and changed the straw in the stalls.

But life at Grandmother Seale's was not all work. A short walk from the house, the children played along the sandy beaches and swam in the blue Caribbean all year long.

By 1934, the Great Depression was deepening in America. Ruby and Charles St. Hill were far from the goals that they had set for themselves seven years earlier. Nevertheless, they knew that they had to bring their children home again. The family had been

A panoramic view of the "Little Scotland" district on the east coast of Barbados.

separated for too long. None of the children had seen their youngest sister, Selma, born while they were in Barbados.

Once again Ruby St. Hill went by ship to the Caribbean. It was a bittersweet visit. Shirley, Odessa, and Muriel always knew that one day they would go back to Brooklyn. The two older girls especially longed to see their parents again. But the island had been their home for almost as long as Shirley and Odessa could remember. All they knew about Brooklyn was that it was very different from their beautiful island. For Grandmother Seale, this was a parting that touched her more than any other. This time she knew that she was saying good-bye to her daughters and grandchildren for the last time. Aunt Violet was taking her children home also. At Grandmother's age, she might not live long enough to see them again.

Women carrying poultry to market in Barbados in the 1920's.

After the endless summer of the island, with its space and sunny beaches, Brooklyn was an abrupt change. That first winter, they shivered in a cold-water apartment. Its only heat came from a kitchen coal stove. Shirley could not get used to the crush of people outside the stores along Pitkin Avenue in the crowded Brownsville neighborhood. Many times she was scolded for stepping into the street where there was more room to walk.

At P.S. 84, the principal and teachers did not know what to do with Shirley. Although she had been successful in the sixth form at her British school, she knew nothing about American history or geography. No one cared that she had learned British history. On her first day, Shirley found herself in a third-grade class with children two or three years younger than she was. Even though she was small for her age, Shirley stood out from the other children. She could read and write better than any of her classmates and she resented being in the same class with them. Shirley finished every assignment first. She tried to be quiet, the way she knew she should. But it was impossible! While the younger children were laboring over their work, she made spitballs and practiced throwing them. That got her teacher's attention! The principal assigned another teacher to coach her in history and geography until she caught up to her grade level.

Although money was still scarce, Ruby and Charles had not forgotten their dreams. They continued to save for a house of their own and the girls' college education. But Ruby did not want her daughters to go without the extras that other children had. She walked a long way to fabric stores that sold the best dressmaking materials at the lowest prices. That way she saved money for her customers. The very best buys were on remnants, small leftover pieces. Remnants were big enough to make dresses for the girls. They always had the prettiest dresses at parties. Ruby sewed the girls' dresses while they slept, after she had finished working for her customers. She and Charles bought a used piano with twenty-five dollars from their savings when Shirley was old enough for lessons.

Shirley and her sisters continued to be best friends the way they had been on the island. Aunt Violet's family lived nearby, and on weekends the cousins all played together.

At the almost all-white school that she attended in the predominantly white neighborhood, Shirley had little sense of racial prejudice. Although she knew that her skin was a different color from that of the other children, it didn't seem to matter. Her arm was raised to answer questions in class as often as any white child's. Her parents' love helped her to love herself. It protected her, when she was young, from many hidden cruelties that surfaced later on.

Saturdays and Sundays in Brooklyn followed a pattern. In the 1930's, children could spend an entire day at the movies for a dime. They lined up early in the morning with lunch in a brown bag to wait for the theater to open. After everyone was seated, the lights dimmed and a series of animated cartoons began. The cartoons were followed by "coming attractions" for movies that would appear the following week. Chapters of serialized adventures came next. By then the audience was in an uproar. Ushers and matrons with flashlights patrolled the aisles. They commanded everyone to stay in their seats and threatened to remove the worst offenders. Each of the two feature films lasted about two hours.

Shirley and her sisters were fascinated with the make-believe world of the movies. Sometimes they completely lost track of time and stayed long after all the other children had gone home. Once, the feature film had begun for the second time when their worried mother came to bring them home.

Almost all of Sunday was spent in prayer at the English Brethren Church. The little church reminded Ruby St. Hill of the faith and British culture that she had learned as a young child in the West Indies. Every Sunday the family walked to three separate services. Both morning and evening worship lasted more than an hour. The afternoon service was Bible Study.

Dressed in their best clothes, Shirley and her sisters had to pass their friends who were out playing. That was the hardest part. If only their mother wasn't so strict! Not just on Sunday, but every day, their friends had different rules to follow. The other children were allowed to cross more streets, and they didn't have to study so much. It wasn't easy being a St. Hill girl, Shirley decided.

On the last day of school in June, the three older girls raced home, eager to show their mother their report cards. She studied each one carefully, praised their successes and urged them to do better the following year. They all wanted her to be proud of them and promised to work harder.

After the school clothes were folded away for that first summer in Brooklyn, Mrs. St. Hill announced a surprise for the next day. They were going to meet Aunt Violet and her children and take a long subway ride together to Coney Island.

The girls were happy to play again in the sand and water. Of course it was crowded in a way that the Barbados beaches had never been. They squeezed into a tiny space with their beach blanket touching the ones on either side.

Mrs. St. Hill resolved to come earlier the next week. That way they'd get a better spot, closer to the water. And they did. Every fine Saturday that summer and the summers that followed, she got up before the girls to get ready. She packed lunch, towels, extra shirts, and sand toys for the little ones. Everyone had something to carry. Charles St. Hill and Uncle Clement missed the days at the beach because Saturday was a working day.

Two years after the return to Brooklyn, the St. Hills moved. Their new home was an apartment with steam heat. On the second floor, over a candy store, it was located in another section of Brooklyn, called Bedford-Stuyvesant. More black people lived in the new neighborhood than in the old. For the first time, Shirley heard racist remarks from white children. A boy in her class told her that his mother didn't allow him to play with "niggers." Although Shirley had never heard the word before, she recognized its hateful meaning the first time it was hurled at her.

Charles and Ruby St. Hill knew that they did not want *their* children with such ignorant and cruel people. Charles advised the bewildered girls to spend more time on their homework and to stick together. He urged them to study hard and do their best in school. The sisters tried not to pay attention to the mean words they heard.

Charles St. Hill had taken a job in a burlap factory at a higher rate of pay. However, the hours were uncertain and he actually brought home less money. His wife knew that she had to help out. She went to work as a maid for a family in Flatbush. To get to work on time, she had to take an early morning subway train. For the first time since they started school in Brooklyn, she was not there to give the children lunch, or to greet them when they came home from school. Shirley, as the oldest, was both the guardian of the house key and of her sisters. She wore the key on a string around her neck. Twice a day, at lunchtime and at dismissal, she walked from her junior high school to her sisters' school. There she picked up the younger girls and walked them home.

The St. Hill girls looked after each other as their parents expected. But soon Shirley would make her first break from the tight little circle of home and sisters. In 1939, she graduated from the neighborhood junior high school and started high school, a bus ride away.

2

Learning, Growing

New York City students can attend either a neighborhood high school or one that offers special programs. Many students travel long distances on buses and subways to their schools. The school that Shirley and her parents chose was Girls' High School in Bedford-Stuyvesant. Its high standards attracted students from all sections of Brooklyn. Shirley made new friends in high school and went to parties and dances. Still, she was bound by her parents' strict rules and early curfew. Her mother refused to listen when she asked to stay out as late as her friends. Ruby was determined that the St. Hill girls would "grow up to be something."

A short time after Shirley entered Girls' High, the family moved to an apartment nearer the school. Her father was hired as the building janitor. Instead of a salary for maintaining the building, the family received a rent-free apartment. Charles St. Hill continued to work at the burlap factory, and Shirley's mother was able to give up her housekeeping job. Instead, Ruby St. Hill stayed home and helped take care of the building.

At Girls' High School, Shirley was elected vice-president of Arista, the honor society, and she won the French medal at graduation. Her excellent academic record earned her scholarship offers from Vassar College and Oberlin College. The St. Hills knew that scholarships were a great honor. Although scholarship funds paid for college tuition, they did not, however, cover many other expenses. Shirley would still have to pay for a room at college, her food, and books. She would also need money to travel to an out-of-town school.

Shirley knew that she could not accept the scholarships. She would go to college—there was no question about that. But she would go to a college that her parents could afford.

Girls' High School, Brooklyn, as it looked when Shirley Chisholm was a student, 1938-1942.

In September 1942, Shirley enrolled at Brooklyn College, a bus ride away in Flatbush. One of five excellent, tuition-free colleges, Brooklyn College admitted high-achieving students from the five boroughs of New York City. Like Shirley, its students were poor, bright, and ambitious.

In the 1940's few career options were open to women, particularly black women. Women were expected to marry, have children and take care of their families. In the years before marriage, they worked at jobs that had little significance. Their real work was thought to start after they married.

Shirley's parents were unusual in expecting their daughters to complete a college education. In contrast to men, fewer women than men graduated from four-year colleges. Even with college degrees, women's career options were limited. Since they were expected to marry and leave work to raise families, they were treated differently from men.

With few exceptions, bright young women who graduated from college became nurses or teachers. Since nursing-school students were required to live at school, they could not accept part-time jobs. Thus nursing was often beyond the reach of poor families. Teaching attracted the best and the brightest.

Although Shirley hadn't quite made up her mind, it was practical for her to consider becoming a teacher. Nevertheless, the interest in politics that would chart another direction began at Brooklyn College.

She had already learned about politics from her father and his friends. Charles St. Hill had left school in fifth grade, but his education had never ended. Each day he read two or three newspapers. Years ago, when people did not own television sets, much more visiting and talk occurred among families and friends. Shirley's father was part of a group of men who enjoyed gathering together. They retold stories of their homeland in the Caribbean and discussed the politics of the day. As a child, Shirley had lain awake many times listening to their conversations.

When the talk turned to politics, Charles St. Hill spoke of Marcus Garvey. Garvey, a black separatist, dreamed of returning American blacks to Africa. He advocated racial purity and believed in keeping the races separate. Long before it was a popular idea, he appealed to black pride. Charles St. Hill read everything about Garvey that he could find.

Shirley Chisholm receiving the Distinguished Alumnae Award of Teachers College, Columbia University, May 15, 1989.

Garvey argued against the ideas of W. E. B. Du Bois, another prominent black leader. Du Bois was the first American black to receive a Ph.D. (Doctor of Philosophy) degree from Harvard University. A scholar who traveled widely, Du Bois was well known for his essays and speeches that called for first-class citizenship for blacks. He was one of the founders of the National Association for the Advancement of Colored People (NAACP). Du Bois believed in bringing blacks into the mainstream of American society. He promoted racial integration to bring black and white people closer together. He wanted them to live peacefully together in the same neighborhoods. He wanted equal job opportunities. Some of the St. Hill friends preferred Du Bois' ideas. The arguments on both sides of the issue continued far into the night in the St. Hill kitchen.

Until the 1960's, laws existed in the United States that prevented black people from enjoying the same rights as whites. In many states, restaurants and hotels could refuse to serve black people. And blacks had to ride in the back of buses and were expected to give up their seats to whites. Public waiting rooms at bus depots and railroad stations had separate areas for blacks and whites, with even drinking fountains labeled for whites or blacks only. These practices that kept the two races separate were part of a system called segregation.

Even in states and cities where no such laws existed, longstanding practices excluded blacks from many opportunities. In neighborhoods where blacks and whites lived together, invisible but powerful racial lines separated them. As a child and later as a teenager, Shirley St. Hill had followed the example of her parents and older cousins. They had accepted the two separate worlds of black and white people. She had her own sisters, cousins, and friends, and there were parties and dances to attend with them. But at Brooklyn College she began to see the society in which she lived from a totally different perspective.

Dozens of campus organizations reached out for members. In

addition to the subject-area clubs that she was familiar with from high school, there were political and social groups. Among the social groups were local chapters of national sororities and fraternities. The national organizations had rules that prevented blacks or Jews from joining them. The local chapters were required to follow the same rules. Brooklyn College students responded by forming mini-fraternities known as "house plans." But even in these groups members decided who could join. Only about sixty of the thousands of students who attended Brooklyn College when Shirley entered were black. In a short time, she had met all of them. Left out of the white students' sororities, fraternities, and house plans, they formed their own groups.

Just as the other students sat with their fraternity and house plan members in the cafeteria, the black students clustered at tables together. The year before Shirley went to Brooklyn College, they had started the Harriet Tubman Society. Shirley joined the Tubman Society in her sophomore year.

The Tubman members followed current news of the city and the country, discussing the effect of political events on black people. They were familiar with prominent black Americans and with their African and American heritages. Shirley again heard the names of people whom she had learned about when her father's friends gathered in the St. Hill kitchen. They were names that she had never heard in high school. High-school history courses covered all the important white Americans but they ignored all but a few prominent blacks.

Shirley's friends had done their own reading to learn about black history. They understood the conflicting ideas of W. E. B. DuBois and Marcus Garvey. They had read Frederick Douglass's writings from a hundred years earlier. As a child living in slavery, Douglass had to exert great effort to learn how to read. After a carefully planned escape to the North when he was a young man, he became a powerful anti-slavery speaker. Later he published an important newspaper and became a consultant to President Lincoln. The students also learned about other heroes, such as Robert Smalls, who piloted a Northern ship during the Civil War.

The Tubman Society particularly acknowledged Shirley's own heroine, Harriet Tubman. Tubman had escaped from slavery almost a hundred years earlier and made her way to the North. In the years before the Civil War began, she had risked her life to return south and bring other slaves to freedom in the North. The black students celebrated Tubman for her courage in war and peace. They were proud that she had insisted on her rights to a pension in return for her wartime service to the Union Army.

In the 1940's, when Shirley was in college, the United States was fighting another war, World War II. Once more, black men served their country in segregated units, separate from white soldiers, sailors, and marines. After fighting in other wars, black men had come home to the same segregation and discrimination that they had left. The Tubman students wanted equality this time for returning black servicemen. The servicemen were risking their lives for democracy; they deserved its fullest measure in return.

Shirley studied her African heritage for the first time. Until then, she had known little of her people before they came to America. In African history and literature, she found accounts of the strength and fortitude of her race. Books on African topics were hard to find, but she shared the ones she found with her Tubman Society friends.

Both in political science courses and in the Political Science Society, Shirley sharpened her public-speaking skills. Her interest in history and politics helped her as a debater. She carefully prepared her arguments and delivered them confidently. She never had to hesitate to choose the right word or think of a response. Her thoughts flowed fluently and swiftly. A petite young woman, she seemed taller when speaking to a group. Imitating Grandmother Seale's erect posture that she had seen as a little girl had given

Shirley the habit of standing very straight. With her head held high, she was a powerful debater.

Louis Warsoff, a blind political science professor, enjoyed talking politics with her. She knew that he respected her opinions. His respect was the first that she had ever sensed from a white person and it made him easy to talk to. Often she stayed after class wanting to learn even more from him. In one of their conversations, after Shirley's success in a debate, he asked about her plans. Would she consider going into politics, he wondered? Her response was definite and realistic.

"You forget two things," she said. "I'm black and I'm a woman."

"You really have deep feelings about that, haven't you?" he murmured. Shirley's deep feelings sprang from years of learning the obstacles to her ambitions. But she *was* interested in politics. If it weren't for the barriers to women and blacks, she would have been more active politically.

After freshman year, she handled both a full course load and a number of outside activities. In addition to her work in the Tubman Society and the Political Science Society, she volunteered her service to the community. In an Urban League settlement house, she conducted arts-and-crafts and sewing classes for children. She also produced skits and plays for them. Caring for her younger sisters had helped her to understand children and she began to think seriously about teaching as a career.

Her college activities, however, fueled her political interest by bringing her into the community. City officials, councilmen, and representatives to the state Assembly came to speak at programs sponsored by the Political Science Society. In the discussions that followed the speeches, Shirley learned how decisions were made in city government. She learned about the influence that local groups had on those decisions. With friends from the Political Science and Tubman Societies, she decided to find out more about local politics. The students began to attend meetings in their own neighborhoods.

Shirley was first drawn to meetings near her home in Bedford-Stuyvesant when city councilmen and department commissioners came to speak. The seating patterns at those meetings reflected society in the 1940's, with separate sections for black and whites. In the question-and-answer periods that followed the officials' prepared talks, few questions were asked. This surprised Shirley, since the meetings were supposed to examine neighborhood problems.

The corner of Fulton Street and Nostrand Avenue in the Bedford-Stuyvesant section of Brooklyn during the 1950's. The empty trash cans signal a recent garbage pick-up; yet the streets are littered.

Blacks in particular said little, afraid to demand the services to which they were entitled. Fear of people who controlled their lives, such as employers who resented troublemakers, kept them quiet. But as a student, Shirley had nothing to lose. As she continued to attend the meetings, she knew that certain questions should be asked. When the sanitation commissioner came, she was ready for him. After his speech, Shirley stood up to be recognized. She wanted to know why trash was not collected regularly in Bedford-Stuyvesant, as it was in white neighborhoods. Why was Bedford-Stuyvesant treated differently? Both the commissioner and the people who ran the meeting were astonished. So was the audience. A buzz went through the gathering. People wanted to know who this little woman was with the big voice. And with the right questions!

Shirley went to more meetings and felt her confidence growing. She made it a point to ask questions, encouraging the neighborhood people to follow her lead.

In her senior year at Brooklyn College, her hairdresser introduced her to a man named Wesley McDonald Holder. Mac, as he was known, was a former editor of the *Amsterdam News*, a black New York newspaper. Active in politics since the 1930's, he wanted to elect more black officials. Mac knew that too many black communities were still represented by white leaders. He also knew that tremendous efforts would be required to elect blacks. Shirley liked what she heard about him. He was trying to make the same kind of changes that she wanted.

The small, trim man had big plans for Bedford-Stuyvesant, or "Bed-Stuy" as it was sometimes called. He told Shirley that everything started in the neighborhoods. She liked the way he urged people to speak out. He told them not to worry about losing their jobs. He said they were only asking for what was due them. Mac was a voice of the future, and when she met him, Shirley was ready to hear it—and act.

3

Teaching

In 1946, Shirley St. Hill graduated from Brooklyn College with a degree in sociology. Her parents rejoiced with her, knowing that the words "cum laude" next to her name meant "with honor." It was their second dream to come true. A year earlier, they had fulfilled their first dream by moving the family into a home of their own on Prospect Avenue in Bedford-Stuyvesant.

Shirley believed that teaching would be her life's work. Her role model was Mary McLeod Bethune. As a young woman teaching in the South in the early part of the twentieth century, Mrs. Bethune had set her sights high. She saw that black children were not being well educated in the segregated schools of Florida. They attended for only a few grades. In a shack near the beach at Daytona, she started a school for girls. The children of the black railroad workers attended elementary and high school there. The school later became Bethune-Cookman College, with Mrs. Bethune as its president.

During the Great Depression of the 1930's, Mrs. Bethune was called to Washington, D.C. As Director of Minority Affairs at the National Youth Affairs department, she began a tutoring program. Black teenagers and college students taught young children to read.

In schools without walls, without a curriculum to follow, they taught about one million children. Although she had never been elected to office, Mrs. Bethune was a public figure. She was a friend of Eleanor Roosevelt, the president's wife, and her advice was sought by the president himself. In San Francisco Mrs. Bethune had attended the first planning meeting of the new United Nations Organization. Shirley liked to read her opinions and activities as they were reported in the newspapers. Mrs. Bethune believed that education would bring real equality to blacks.

Before she graduated from Brooklyn College, Shirley fell in love. Although she was engaged to be married, she did not think of a job as a period of marking time before marriage. She had prepared herself to teach and looked forward to her first job.

But the first job did not come easily. World War II had just ended and Shirley found few openings for teachers in that first peacetime year. During the war, vacancies had occurred when teachers were drafted into the armed services. Appointments to fill their places were made from the long list of teachers who had waited through the Depression for jobs. When the war ended, returning teachers went back to their classrooms. Nevertheless, Shirley made the rounds of the schools. She tracked down every opening, followed up every lead. The principals who interviewed her were not encouraging. They could easily find experienced teachers. If they hired a new graduate, they wanted someone who appeared stronger, someone taller. Small and slender, Shirley did not look old enough to teach. But her persistence was rewarded when she finally landed her first job as a teacher's aide. Mt. Calvary Child Care Center in Harlem was willing to take a chance on the new graduate.

Eager to grow professionally, Shirley continued to study. Teachers College of Columbia University was a short distance from the child-care center. It was famous for its program in early childhood education. Shirley enrolled in the master's degree program. After the children at Mt. Calvary Child Care Center went

Shirley in 1950 in the St. Hill home at age 26.

home for the day, she went to her classes in the old Gothic-style building on West 120th Street.

Each night she listened to lectures on the theories of teaching young children. With her fellow students, she explored research on early childhood education. Long hours in the library and reading at home kept her current with class assignments. And every day there were the children to teach. She could still remember how much she had learned as a four-year-old in her first days of school in Barbados. Shirley was anxious to take advantage of the little children's intense curiosity and desire to learn.

She was busy, happy, and—in love. Her first romance was with an older man she had met while still at Brooklyn College. He was attentive in a way she had never experienced with boys her own age. The young men she knew thought she was too intellectual. Shirley and her sisters attended many neighborhood dances while they were in high school and college. These were sponsored by local adult social clubs. Shirley loved to dance and attracted lots of partners. Quick and graceful, she always knew the latest steps for the Lindy, one of the new dances that grown-ups called jitterbugging. But she was only fun to talk to until the topic got serious. When she turned the conversation to world events, boys looked for reasons to get away. They were uncomfortable with this bright young woman who challenged them to think. And Shirley wasn't content with the light talk that the boys were interested in.

But the older man, who came from the Caribbean island of Jamaica, was different. She had met him during Easter vacation of her senior year at Brooklyn College, when she worked in a jewelry factory. She brought him home to meet the family. Dressed in stylish comfort, he wore his shirt open under a jacket. Shirley's mother had very definite ideas about how a man should dress when he called on a young lady. It bothered her that he came to the house without a tie. Terribly hurt by her mother's dislike, Shirley defended him and continued to see him. The relationship created a serious conflict in the family. Shirley felt that her mother was old-fashioned and had judged him unfairly. Although she knew that both parents would have liked her to date someone closer to her own age, she hoped that, in time, she would win them over.

But the man that Shirley thought she knew so well never really existed. In his place, she found a totally different man from the one she thought she knew. First he was charged with immigration fraud, then she learned that he already had a wife and family in Jamaica. His deceit, arrest, and deportation from the country shocked Shirley and her family.

Her hurt was so intense that she thought she would never care for another man again. She made herself concentrate completely on the little children she taught. They would have all her love, she decided. She determined to devote her life to teaching, and never marry.

4

Speaking Out

But Conrad Chisholm, whom Shirley had met the year before at Columbia University, had other plans. As soon as he heard that her engagement was broken, Conrad asked for a date. Each time that she refused, he asked again. His friendly interest was impossible to discourage. And after a while, she no longer wanted to discourage him. She found herself attracted to the persistent, smiling Conrad. Also from Jamaica and nine years older than Shirley, he was in every other way different from her first fiancé.

Shirley's mother immediately liked the new boyfriend despite the age difference. The rest of the family liked him too. Shirley and Conrad were married in 1949 and moved into an apartment in Bedford-Stuyvesant.

Shirley continued to teach at the Mt. Calvary Day Care Center and attend her graduate-school classes. Even with more things to do, she still found time for politics. Conrad worked for a private security agency that specialized in insurance claims for disability cases. When his schedule permitted, he went with Shirley to political meetings.

In 1951, Shirley received her Master of Arts degree in early

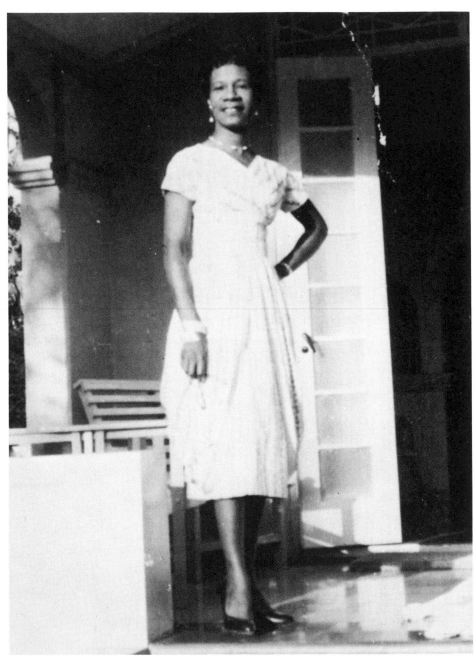

Shirley on a visit to Saratoga Springs, New York, around 1954.

childhood education from Columbia University. With four years of day-care experience and her new degree, she was ready for the next stage in her career. The following year, she became the director of a private nursery school in Brooklyn. As director, she could put into practice the research and teaching strategies that she had learned in graduate school. Then, after a year in the new position, she was appointed director of a large child-care center. Located on the Lower East Side of Manhattan, Hamilton-Madison Child Care Center was across the East River, a subway ride away from Brooklyn. As director, she supervised a staff of thirty-four and administered a program for 130 children. With each step in her career, she influenced an increasing number of teachers and children.

Meanwhile, Shirley stayed active in local politics. In New York City when she was growing up, political clubs dominated politics. These powerful groups were organized in every Assembly district. Each district elected a representative to the New York State Assembly, where state laws were passed. Sometimes the club leader was the elected assemblyman from the district. Since the Democrats were in the majority in New York City, the most active clubs were run by Democrats.

Regular club members worked hard to elect the people they favored. Club workers knew everyone in the district. They did favors for the local residents and encouraged them to vote with the party. Not only assemblymen, but other city, state, and national candidates were supported by the local groups.

The old regulars at the clubhouse were trying to hold fast to their positions of power. Openings that occurred on the board were still filled with whites. But local politics in Brooklyn were about to change. Shirley St. Hill Chisholm would play a major role in that change.

On Monday and Thursday nights, people came to the political clubhouse with their problems. Someone there could usually help. The clubs were originally formed to welcome new immigrants.

During the nineteenth century and the early years of the twentieth, large numbers of immigrants poured into New York. For these newcomers, the clubs offered many different services. It was there that immigrants learned about American customs. They were helped to find construction jobs and work on the docks. Later, they learned about taking tests to become police officers, fire fighters, and garbage collectors. Clubhouse lawyers gave free legal advice. The needy received Thanksgiving turkeys and other donations of food and clothing.

Political club members helped the immigrants to become citizens. Once sworn in, the new citizens were shown how to register to vote. Club members were not just ready to help, they were anxious to dispense favors. They fostered the feeling that an obligation had been incurred. It was no secret that a vote for the club candidates fulfilled the obligation.

Leaders of the Seventeenth Assembly District Democratic club in the Chisholms' district were still all white, even though blacks had lived in the district since the 1930's. With the World War II surge, the district population was two-thirds black by the end of the 1940's. Although black people came to the clubhouse meetings, they were not part of the organization. They came because they needed help. Their votes were welcome. But, beyond that, the organization had little interest in them. They were not allowed to feel as if they belonged. Seating arrangements, with whites on one side of the aisle and blacks on the other, were strictly enforced. No one could speak unless recognized. A club member would tap someone in the audience on the shoulder. The tap granted permission to ask a question. Black people were afraid to complain in public sessions about the lack of services. They asked only for things they needed personally.

The white leaders in Brooklyn Democratic politics had no intention of sharing their power with the new majority. The old clubhouse regulars held fast to their positions. Whenever openings occurred on the governing board of the club, they were invariably filled by whites. At the end of the decade, Brooklyn still had no black elected official at the city, state, or national level. But outside the clubhouse the black population was listening to new voices.

One of those voices was Wesley McDonald Holder. Shirley had first met Mac Holder in 1946 when she was still a student. Because he was also interested in making changes, she began working closely with him. Mac planned to start with the political clubs. He urged black people to join the local organization and make their voices heard. They followed his advice, but the leadership still wasn't listening.

Shirley began to attend the club meetings every week. The little woman with the big voice was now well known. But she soon grew dissatisfied with her role as an outsider. She was tired of waiting in the audience to ask a question. She decided to join the Seventeenth Assembly District Democratic Club as a regular member.

Club leaders were happy to have a hardworking black woman in the group. Her presence made the regular membership look as if it was integrated with both white and black people.

Her first assignment was to the card party committee. All the committee members were women. The annual card party was a big fund raiser and the women took their assignment seriously. A large part of the club's income was derived from card party revenue. The rest came from members' dues. Shirley urged the committee women to make their husbands recognize the event's key role in the club's finances. Every year the women turned back all the proceeds to the club treasury. As they began their work the next year, they had no budget for expenses. Shirley insisted that they ask for start-up funds.

While the women followed her advice, Shirley designed and made table decorations. With inexpensive trim and recycled cigar boxes begged from shopkeepers, she created colorful centerpieces for the card tables.

Shirley learned about politics as a regular club member and as a friend of Wesley McDonald Holder. People like Mac Holder were tired of the silence that surrounded racial discrimination in New York City. Although no laws barred black people from public places, they were kept out in other ways. Brooklyn hotels, for example, refused to rent space to black groups for meetings. Mac decided to start his fight against discrimination with the hotels. In 1948, he succeeded in getting the Towers Hotel to drop the color barrier and host a black fraternity dance.

Next, he turned to the courts. All 49 civil judges in Brooklyn were white. Mac decided that the time had come for a black candidate. He proposed Lewis S. Flagg, Jr. to run for municipal court judge. Following the usual procedure in city politics, he asked the Seventeenth Assembly District to nominate Flagg. As he expected, the district leadership balked and named a white candidate instead. But Mac knew that Flagg could still be nominated outside the regular organization. It meant getting enough support to put Flagg's name on the ballot in the primary election. That way the voters, and not the organization, would decide whether he could run for judge.

A primary election decides who will be the party's candidate. Before the primary, different factions can promote their own candidates. The candidate who wins usually receives the support of the entire party. In many sections of New York City, Democrats get the most votes. Therefore, winning the Democratic Party nomination means getting elected.

Mac formed a committee to nominate Lewis Flagg. Because Flagg was an outstanding lawyer, both blacks and whites joined the committee. Their first task was to get his name on the ballot with a petition signed by voters in the district. Shirley Chisholm canvassed for Flagg, going from door to door in the district. She asked for signatures on Flagg's petition to have his name placed on the ballot for the primary election. After enough signatures were collected and the petition was filed, she went back to the same streets. This time she asked people to vote for Lewis Flagg in the primary election. Door-to-door canvassing and vote-getting were time-consuming, but the extra effort paid off.

Black residents were surprised that one of their group had a chance to win an election. Flagg's supporters provided them with more detailed information than the newspapers did. When they learned about the candidate's qualifications, they were eager to support him. And they were grateful to Shirley and the other workers who took the time to tell them about the campaign. To further push Flagg's candidacy, Mac organized a mail campaign to the entire district.

Efforts to get out the vote succeeded. In 1953, Flagg was elected, the first black judge in Brooklyn history. Shirley knew that the election was a milestone. At the victory celebration, Mac predicted that they would soon see a black city councilman, assemblyman, and congressman representing Bedford-Stuyvesant. In the excitement of victory, Shirley cheered what may have sometimes seemed an impossible dream. She and Mac resolved to keep pushing for broader black representation. As a start, he decided to keep together the group that had elected Flagg. He named the new political club The Bedford-Stuyvesant Political League (BSPL). In the year after Flagg's election, 1954, the BSPL announced a full slate of black candidates. The group proposed names for Congress, the State Senate, district leader, co-leader, and assemblyman. Mac himself was the BSPL candidate for district leader.

Shirley was second in command to Mac in 1954. She had proved herself an intelligent thinker and a hard worker in the Flagg campaign. In turn, she admired Mac's shrewd assessment of political winds and his tremendous organizational powers. He had taken a handful of people and forged them into a band of crusaders. The big question was whether they could do it again. Shirley and everyone else intended to try.

Shirley and her sisters outside the St. Hill house in the 1950's.

BSPL pamphlets reminded voters of their success in electing Judge Flagg. "Make history again!" became their slogan. "The BSPL demands fuller and fairer political representation for Negroes. It supports vigorous militant Negro leadership!"

But it was an uphill struggle from the start. None of the 1954 candidates had Judge Flagg's reputation. In the end, Mac was defeated for district leader and the rest of the slate went down, too.

Although she was disappointed, Shirley knew that in 1954, the regular Democratic Club was still all-powerful. The BSPL could not expect in one election to overthrow its strength, built over many years. She tried not to feel frustrated, even when black voters continued to support the regular Democratic candidates. She knew they were unfamiliar with the new candidates and unwilling to take a chance on them. At the same time, the regular organization candidates had begun to listen to black issues. They knew that to survive, they had to change. In a move to break the BSPL, they ran black candidates themselves and succeeded in splitting the black vote. But, despite its lack of full support, the BSPL persisted. In each of the elections after 1955, the new group took a few more votes away from the Seventeenth District Assembly Democratic Club.

During the 1953-54 campaigns, Shirley was a member both of the BSPL and of the regular Democratic organization, the Seventeenth Assembly District Democratic Club. From the inside, she challenged the regular Democrats to respond to black issues. Hoping to win her over, along with the votes that she drew to BSPL candidates, they elected her to the Board of Directors. It was an unprecedented action on the part of the regular club members. They were taking into their inner circle a black woman still in her twenties.

At Board meetings, Shirley still pointed out the lack of black representation at every level of government. From her seat on the dais at public meetings, she continued to direct difficult questions at visiting speakers. She wanted to know why the housing codes weren't enforced. Landlords in other parts of the city were penalized for violations that were allowed in Bedford-Stuyvesant. Shirley had a list of examples ready to embarrass any official who thought that she was bluffing. Her behavior annoyed the other directors. Board members were expected to remain quiet or to defend guest speakers against criticism that came from the audience.

But if they thought they could quiet her, they were mistaken. The old trick of silencing critics by taking them into the group didn't work with Shirley. It wasn't in her nature to remain silent. The price of silence was too high for the small bit of power that came with being a director. She believed that it was her responsibility as a Board member to represent the people of the district. Bedford-Stuyvesant was still not getting its fair share of city services. She demanded changes that her fellow members saw no reason to make. Finally, they tired of her behavior and voted her off the Board.

The change made no difference to Shirley, but the Board members looked surprised when she appeared at the clubhouse the following week. Perhaps they thought she would be too embarrassed to return. When she saw them nudging one another, she walked to the dais and shook each of their hands. Back in her old place in the audience, she kept her challenges going. In the years that followed, more people joined her in asking the same tough questions. Shirley knew that she had begun to make a difference in her community.

5

Changing the Political Establishment

Not just in her own block and in her church, but all over Bedford-Stuyvesant, people knew Shirley Chisholm. They greeted her by name as she stood in line at stores or waited for buses. At election times, she was a tireless worker. Between campaigns, she reached out to the community. In the National Association of Colored People (NAACP), the League of Women Voters, and the Stuyvesant Community Center, she found forums in which to air her views. Her speeches prompted serious discussion among her listeners. They wondered, as she did, when Bedford-Stuyvesant would receive its fair share of police protection and other city services. Her husband was a perfect sounding board for her ideas and speeches. Proud of his wife, Conrad Chisholm encouraged her political activity.

As Bedford-Stuyvesant Political League vice-president, Shirley Chisholm brought the issues straight to City Hall. She led delegations to the mayor's office, demanding their fair share. On the subway ride to Manhattan, noisy and waving signs, they attracted attention to their cause. At rallies, she criticized city officials and the Democratic Party for ignoring central Brooklyn.

Mac Holder had been president of the BSPL since its formation in 1953. By 1958, some members were ready for a change. Sure that Shirley was a natural candidate for the job, they urged her to run for president of the League. For years, she had worked by his side, getting ready to lead. But she soon discovered that Mac was not ready to step aside.

One of the BSPL members handed Shirley a copy of a pink sheet that was circulating in the club. In it Mac accused her of ingratitude. He denounced her for being too ambitious and stated that she needed more experience. Shirley was astounded that her friend and great political teacher could be so petty. But she wouldn't let him stop her. Confident that she had earned the right to run for president of the BSPL, she decided to let the members decide.

In spite of her determination, Shirley lost the BSPL election. At that moment, both she and Mac lost something more precious— their friendship. The League lost too.

In the 1958 primary fight, Mac did not get the nomination for the State Assembly. Two years later, in another try for the Assembly seat, his nominating petition was struck down. Challenging rival candidates' petitions was a routine political tactic. The regular organization claimed that names on the nominating petition were not from registered voters. Without the challenged names, the candidate did not have enough to make the petition valid. There was rarely time to prove the charges false or to get other names before the filing deadline. Therefore, a petition challenge was a convenient way to keep serious candidates off the ballot.

Mac continued to run BSPL candidates against the Seventeenth Assembly District Democratic Club candidates. His hope was that another BSPL candidate, like Judge Flagg, would win the primary election and become the Democratic candidate in the general election.

But the Bedford-Stuyvesant Political League survived only a few more years, weakened by the bad feelings of the Chisholm-

Holder dispute. Hope of becoming a real challenge to the regular Democrats dimmed. More than ever, blacks and whites both continued to support the candidates of the regular organization, the Seventeenth Assembly District Democratic Club.

Even though the BSPL was active for a short time, its legacy was enormous. Perhaps the most lasting accomplishment, next to Flagg's election, was its success in awakening the political awareness of blacks living in the district. By 1958, its voter registration drives had brought thousands of minority members to the polls. The

Shirley Chisholm as a day-care director in 1950's.

regular party organization could no longer ignore them. Black candidates appeared on the regular Democratic organization slates and, one after another, were elected.

In the wake of her dispute with Mac, Shirley broke with the BSPL. After her resignation in 1958, she concentrated fully on her educational career. She exchanged her political zeal for another crusade. Shirley's speeches demanding quality day care had extended her reputation as an educator beyond the borders of Bedford-Stuyvesant. After setting high standards at the Hamilton-Madison Child Care Center, she was appointed director of the City Division of Day Care in 1959. In her new job, she supervised ten city-run day-care centers with ten directors.

To the public and private centers under her care, Shirley Chisholm brought her own philosophy. She believed in teaching children to read as early as possible. Born of her experience as a child in Barbados, the belief was confirmed in her graduate study at Teachers College. She knew the distinct advantage her early start had given her. Beginning to read and write had made her feel competent when she was only four years old. As a little child, she had come to enjoy learning. She had never feared or avoided it.

"I know that eye muscles are not developed enough for reading or finger muscles are not developed for writing, and I say baloney, because I learned to read when I was three and a half and I learned to write when I was four," she told the directors. If she could acquire those skills and attitudes at such an early age, she believed that city children could, too.

Not everyone agreed with her philosophy of early childhood education. Many educators sincerely believed that children would benefit from a later start in learning to read and write. If the children came from poor homes, some teachers anticipated difficulty and did not try to teach them. Others pitied poor children and refused to make demands on them. Perhaps without meaning to, they deprived the children even more. But Shirley's message was firm and un-

46

yielding. The children under her care deserved the best start. If they came from poor or troubled homes, then the staff had to try even harder to overcome those handicaps.

An important part of her job was convincing community leaders of the need to develop more day-care centers. Women had still not entered the labor market in great numbers in 1959. Therefore, city officials and business leaders saw no need for more day-care centers. However, Shirley and other early childhood educators persevered, knowing how many children were left unsupervised at home already. They were intent on getting quality day care for those children. At this critical time in the children's development, Shirley knew that they needed the best of care. Centers with well-designed programs could offer them a desirable place to stay while their mothers worked.

By thinking ahead, the business and civic leaders could develop first-rate programs. She urged them to aim for the highest standards. Shirley felt like a missionary, spreading the word at endless meetings. For two years, she devoted herself completely to developing programs.

But Shirley knew that she couldn't stay out of politics for long. 1960 was a restless year for New York City Democratic politics. In every county, reform candidates challenged the regular organization. That year, friends asked her to help them start a reform group within the Democratic Party. The early promise of the BSPL had never been fulfilled. Members had drifted away, some back to the regular Democratic organization. But a few of Shirley's friends believed that the time had come to overthrow the entrenched leadership in the Seventeenth Assembly District.

They called their new group the Unity Democratic Club. Members discovered that they had issues in common with a neighboring reform group, the Nostrand Democratic Party. The Nostrand people were not concerned with racial problems, but they were as intent as Unity in getting more services for the neighborhood. They wanted increased police protection, better schools, more youth services, cleaner streets with brighter lights, and improved garbage collection.

Members of both groups saw the advantages of uniting to propose a single slate of candidates. The new group called itself the Unity-Nostrand Democratic Club. Its members nominated Thomas R. Jones, a hardworking black lawyer, for assemblyman. For district leader, they chose a white Nostrand candidate, Joseph K. Rowe. Jones and Rowe ran a campaign that demanded increased city services. They denounced the regular Democratic club as indifferent to the voters' needs.

In the 1960 primary campaign, Shirley put to use all the vote-getting skills that she had learned in the BSPL. She taught Unity-Nostrand volunteers how to canvass for votes and how to gather legal signatures on petitions. She knew how crucial careful organization was. The more voters they contacted personally, the better their chances of winning.

The Unity campaign was loud and visible. Shirley and the other members worked hard to attract well-known names to their cause. In a campaign swing though New York City to support reform candidates, Eleanor Roosevelt spoke at one of their rallies. Four hundred people heard the former president's wife support Jones and Rowe. The popular black singer Harry Belafonte had his name at the top of Unity's letterhead.

On primary days, supporters of each candidate watched the voting places carefully. They wanted to make sure that only registered voters were counted. People known as poll watchers were assigned to each polling, or voting, place. Poll watchers made sure that the rules were observed. Signs and other literature promoting candidates were not allowed. Before voters could enter the voting booth, their names had to be found in the list of registered voters. If they hadn't registered, they weren't allowed to vote.

The Seventeenth Assembly District Democratic Club paid

Mrs. Eleanor Roosevelt, wife of President Franklin D. Roosevelt, in 1960.

members' friends to watch the polls. These poll watchers turned election and primary days into social events. Over coffee and doughnuts they chatted with voters all day long. They weren't always careful about checking the voting lists.

But Shirley knew that every vote was important. Unity chose poll watchers who took their jobs seriously. Unpaid and vigilant Unity workers watched the names on the voter registers and challenged many voters. Their stern behavior made the paid party workers nervous.

The reform vote in the Seventeenth Assembly District was substantial in 1960, but not enough to win. Jones came in second with 42 percent of the vote. Once again, the regular organization seated its candidates.

But Unity had proved itself. Increased voter registration had brought its candidates close to victory. Shirley and the other Unity members knew that they had a winner in Jones. Capable and confident, he inspired black pride in Bedford-Stuyvesant residents.

Immediately after the primary, Unity began to prepare for 1962. Voter registration was the key. Certain that most of the new voters had voted for Unity, Shirley and her organization made plans to increase their registration drive before the next election. They held community meetings to urge active participation in politics. They studied the neighborhoods and their voter registration patterns. One by one, they visited streets with low registration.

Throughout the election district, they sold the message of the Unity Club: Bed-Stuy should choose its own representatives! By 1962, the next election year, Shirley knew that they were ready. That year Unity left the Nostrand coalition. Confident that the district would support black candidates, they ran Jones for both assemblyman and district leader. Ruth Goring was their candidate for co-leader.

The new campaign was even more forceful than the first one in 1960. A flyer urged "End boss-ruled plantation politics!" The

50

liberal New York press objected to the black-versus-white message. But Unity members brushed off the objections. They hadn't seen many editorials that questioned the years of all-white rule. Shirley and the other members pounded home the platform. More jobs in the community's stores and factories! Raise the minimum wage!

The primary fight, which ended in a Unity victory, assured success in the general election, since the Democratic Party held the majority in New York City politics. The Republican Party attracted little support in the Seventeenth Assembly District.

The election-day sweep made Unity the official Democratic club in the Seventeenth Assembly District. Jones won the assembly seat and was elected district leader. He and his co-leader, Ruth Goring, took their seats on the county Democratic committee. They made up two of the four black votes on the twenty-two member committee in 1962. The proportion was still much lower than the black-white ratio of the county population, but it was a beginning.

Shirley emerged from the 1962 election with a seat on the new district committee, the Unity Democratic Club. It was the second time that she had occupied a director's chair in a district organization. When she had been on the board of the old Seventeenth Assembly District, no one had listened to her. But this time, she was an equal partner in the Unity leadership. She guided members with less experience, and club candidates relied on her advice. They counted on her persistence and willingness to work long hours. For more than ten years, she had pounded the streets, climbed stairs, arranged candidates' teas and spoken on their behalf to small and large groups.

But Shirley wanted more. She was ready to claim their support for her leadership.

6

Challenging the Assembly Seat

In 1964, Shirley saw her chance. It was another election year and she was ready for a change.

After Thomas R. Jones' successful term in the New York State Assembly, he could count on reelection. According to party custom, elected officials were nominated for the offices they already held. No one would think of challenging the popular Jones in a primary fight. However, there was a chance that Jones would take himself out of the race.

A position had opened for a civil court judge, and county committee members wanted to nominate Jones for that post. As a capable lawyer and a proven vote-getter, he would strengthen the Democratic ticket.

Jones, a thoughtful, dedicated lawyer, deserved the judicial nomination. Although he wanted the job, he didn't immediately accept the nomination for district judge. As district leader, his first obligation was to the Unity club. Unity members needed another candidate for his Assembly seat—a winning candidate. If they didn't have one, the club could lose its official status.

Shirley saw no reason for Jones to decline the nomination for the Brooklyn court. Unity had another winning candidate for his Assembly seat, an experienced, dedicated, and deserving candidate—Shirley Chisholm. She believed that her allegiance to other people's campaigns for more than a decade had earned her their votes.

But some of the men who had worked alongside her in the campaigns and who sat beside her on the Unity Executive Board hesitated. A woman? A black woman? Bedford-Stuyvesant send a black woman to the Assembly? Why they had just succeeded in

Assemblywoman Shirley Chisholm with Mrs. Mildred Epps and Judge Thomas R. Jones.

electing the first black man to that body! And if they couldn't imagine Shirley as a candidate, what would other voters think? They were convinced that she would attract few votes.

During a meeting at Jones's house, called to resolve the dispute, he again expressed his indecision. Deeply hurt, Shirley realized that some club members were trying to block her nomination.

"If you need to have a discussion, have a discussion. But it makes no difference to me," she cried out in anger. "I intend to fight!"

The club members finally agreed to give her the nomination. Many of them made no secret of their hope that Jones would change his mind before he officially accepted the judicial nomination.

After Jones announced her as Unity's choice, there was more debate. County officials objected to running a woman. Everyone knew that politics was a man's job. And what they knew about this particular woman wasn't good. Scrappy, too independent and too quick to speak her mind. In the Assembly she might be more trouble to her own party than the opposition!

Even after Unity endorsed Shirley, Jones continued to delay his acceptance. People were urging him to reclaim his right to the Assembly nomination. But Jones wanted to be a judge, and finally he became a candidate for the civil court. The way was clear for Shirley Chisholm.

Conrad Chisholm, Shirley's husband, supported her completely. If that's what she wanted to do, he would help her. Whenever he could, he was by her side as she toured the neighborhoods, asking for votes.

On one of their tours through a housing project, an older man refused to shake Shirley's outstretched hand.

"Young woman," he demanded. "What are you doing out here in the cold? Did you get your husband's breakfast this morning? Did you straighten up your house? What are you doing running for office? That is something for men."

Conrad knew that he could never make the older man understand that he and Shirley were happy together. Shirley had never
disappointed him. They had a lovely, comfortable apartment, but it
didn't require full-time care. He had never expected Shirley to stay
home when he was capable of taking care of himself. Actually, they
spent a great deal of time together when he wasn't traveling on
business. His work as a private investigator with the railroads often
took him out of town. But when he was home, Conrad joined Shirley
in canvassing votes for Unity candidates. He admired his wife's
dedication to politics. He knew that she had a gift of leadership and
that he would be selfish to prevent her from using it for the good of
other people. After two miscarriages, Shirley and Conrad knew they
could not have children. Shirley's energies were directed toward
helping other people's children, first as an educator and later as a
political figure.

The older man's outburst at the housing project, which took
them both by surprise, was not the last one they heard. For every
person who disliked the idea of a black person running for office,
more objected to a woman. For some people, it still was not a
woman's job.

Shirley realized that she was particularly unpopular with black
men. Generations of black men had been unable to participate fully
in American society. The barriers they had faced kept them from
adequately caring for their families. Black women had to help
support the families. Often there were more jobs for women, such
as housework, than there were for men. But the men didn't want to
acknowledge that they needed the help. Instead, they tried to deny
it. The idea of black women entering politics before black men had
been fully accepted in that arena was a terrible blow. Shirley
understood the problem, but it wasn't going to stop her.

Knowing that she wouldn't persuade many men, she made
special appeals to black women. Shirley knew their special needs
and concerns. She talked to them as they stood in line at the

supermarkets. On street corners, at community meetings and coffees, she listened to their problems and promised to work hard to solve them. They wanted safe streets, better schools and playgrounds free of danger. They wanted to shop in supermarkets with the same low prices charged in other neighborhoods. And they wanted the stores on Pitkin Avenue to carry items of good quality. They were tired of having no selection and having to pay high prices for cheap clothing and furniture.

An historic Supreme Court decision earlier in 1964 had changed the face of district politics. The decision worked to Shirley's advantage. Brooklyn congressional districts had been drawn in such a way as to protect the people in office from any serious challenge. The practice was called gerrymandering. Gerrymandering cut up black neighborhoods, assigning them to several adjacent districts that had large white populations. One black leader compared the gerrymandering with the more open Southern efforts to keep blacks out of power. "The result," he said, "is that black men in both cases are governed by white men." The Supreme Court decision, by requiring a one-man, one-vote rule, called for new district lines. The old lines that split black communities and kept them from having a majority were erased. For the first time, communities elected representatives who would work for their needs. Bedford-Stuyvesant was an intact assembly district, no longer split three ways. Shirley ran for a seat that would represent the whole Bedford-Stuyvesant community.

Shirley easily won the Democratic primary in September of 1964. Unity's intense voter registration drive and her direct appeal to women paid off. In the November election she received ten times more votes than her Republican rival. She would be the only black woman in the 188th session of the New York State Assembly. Five other black assemblymen were elected as well as two state senators.

In the excitement of winning her first public office, Shirley had one deep regret. Her father had not lived to enjoy her victory. A year

Members of Shirley Chisholm's family in the 1950's. Her father, Charles St. Hill, mother Ruby, and sister Odessa with her husband.

earlier, he had come in from working in his sunny backyard, complaining to her mother of a headache. Charles St. Hill sat down and died quietly of a stroke.

The man who was so proud of his close family unintentionally divided it. In his will he left the house on Prospect Avenue to his wife and three younger daughters. He singled out Shirley by leaving her all his savings, knowing that she would need money for her political campaigns. The rest of the family resented her, even though she had known nothing about her father's will.

The St. Hills were never again the same close family after Charles St. Hill's death. Shirley had only Conrad to share her election victory. When she left to take her seat in the New York State Legislature, none of the St. Hill family was there to see her off.

7

Assemblywoman Chisholm

One cold day in January 1965, Conrad and a group of friends went to Grand Central Terminal in New York City with Shirley. They had come to see her off on the train to Albany. She left with high hopes, ready to address the needs of the ordinary people whom she would represent in the New York State Legislature. She could hardly wait to get started.

The old legislative building itself was intimidating. Built in the nineteenth century, its twin towers dominated the gray January sky. On the first day of the legislative session, its great caverns of empty space filled with milling crowds. Like other new legislators, Shirley followed its maze of marble-lined corridors, trying to find her way to the Assembly chamber. Fortunately, guards were posted, directing the way for newcomers.

The Assembly and the Senate made up the two houses of the New York State Legislature. Representatives from every district in the state met together for the two years of their terms as assemblymen. Each year a new session began. During that time, they worked on small committees and prepared bills to introduce to the full body for a vote.

Before the business of the legislative session began, however, each house had to elect a leader. In the Assembly, the leader was known as the Speaker. The Speaker's job was powerful. He made appointments to committees and decided which bills would be brought to the whole Assembly for a vote. Following a longtime custom, the Speaker came from the majority party. The Assembly had been Republican for eight years prior to the new session. But the Supreme Court ruling that had redrawn district lines had made a Democratic majority possible. The new Speaker would be a Democrat and the Democrats should have been ready to elect a Speaker. Normally, a new Assembly spent thirty minutes or less choosing its leader.

One choice, a natural one, was Anthony Travia, an assemblyman from Brooklyn. In the eight years when the Republicans controlled the Assembly, Travia had been minority leader. He had served the party well and expected to be chosen as Speaker.

However, he was challenged by another Brooklyn assemblyman, Stanley Steingut. Steingut was the Brooklyn county chairman and the son of Irwin Steingut, an earlier Speaker of the Assembly. Steingut claimed a natural right to the post.

When the Assembly gathered on the first morning of the session, the rumors favored Steingut's election. In fact, he had many votes promised to him. Most of the Brooklyn delegation supported him. And he also had support from Democratic assemblymen from other parts of the city and state. But Anthony Travia had many votes promised to him too. Enough votes to worry Steingut. None of the Democrats wanted to take a vote while they were split. With a split, and the Republican minority voting for its own choice, no one would get a majority. While the vote was in question, no Assembly business took place. Although members gathered in the green-carpeted Assembly chamber each day, the group was not officially convened. In the evening, the two candidates received guests at separate suites in the Hotel De Witt Clinton. Travia supporters visited the Travia suite. Steingut's went to Steingut's suite.

Shirley Chisholm did not make a call at either suite. She saw no reason for the dispute. Although she didn't know Anthony Travia very well, she asked more experienced assemblymen about him. He was hard working, they told her, staying long hours to study bills. He was in his office every morning at 8 A.M., before the cleaning ladies had gone home. He had led the Assembly effectively during the Republican years, she discovered. No one could think of anything unfavorable to report about him. Although some legislators used their public office as a means of attracting business to their law firms, Travia had not. His firm was even smaller than when he was first elected to the Assembly in 1942.

The whole dispute, from what Shirley could see, stemmed from Stanley Steingut's ambition. He wanted the job and didn't care how he got it. She was ready to cast her vote for Travia. She believed that Travia had earned the Speaker's post. But despite all the begging for votes around her, no one asked about hers. Everyone assumed that the new assemblywoman from Brooklyn would follow her county leader. Steingut thought he had her vote. She was not invited to any of the frequent strategy meetings where ways to break the deadlock were discussed. Representatives on both sides of the feud thought they knew Shirley's mind. No one ever missed her at the evening gatherings in Steingut's suite.

Shirley grew impatient with the long delay but there was nothing she could do but wait. While the fight for the Speaker's post continued into February, Assembly business did not take place. No committee appointments were made. No committees met. No legislation was proposed. The Assembly was at a standstill. Its members came together each day only to decide whether to take a vote.

Each weekend Shirley went home to Brooklyn and Conrad. The following Monday she returned to Albany. Daily she crisscrossed the path between her hotel room and the legislative building. Rumors flew among the legislators. At times Steingut seemed certain to win. But almost immediately, they'd hear that Travia was ahead.

One day another legislator from Brooklyn casually remarked to Shirley that she couldn't go wrong with a vote for Steingut. "Who told you I was going to vote for Stanley?" she asked. The legislator was shocked. He could not believe that a freshman assemblywoman would bypass the county leader. She explained her conviction about Travia's merit for the post. Seeing her colleague's disbelief, she told him plainly that she'd made up her mind. "Shirley, you're committing political suicide," he warned her.

His meaning was clear. Steingut would owe nothing to those who voted against him. She could expect no help from him if she ever needed it. And perhaps none from her fellow Democratic legislators, either.

The long delay worked against Steingut. Republicans in the Assembly finally tired of the stalemate. They cast their votes with Travia, passing over their own party's candidate. When the vote was called on the night of February 4, he won the Speaker's post. His election came on the twenty-eighth ballot. The thirty-day deadlock was over and Travia was led to the high-backed, red leather speaker's chair. There he gave the gavel a resounding whack to call the Assembly to order. Assembly work officially began the following Monday, five weeks behind schedule.

Travia was as surprised as Steingut with Shirley's vote. In all the Assembly, only he and Shirley knew that she had received no favor in exchange for her vote. But many people who didn't know her very well thought otherwise. Although Shirley's vote actually played no part in the outcome, Steingut now had real cause to dislike the independent little woman from Brooklyn.

Once the Speaker was chosen, the Assembly got to work. Travia did not use committee appointments to reward or punish assemblymen. About half of the committee chairman's appointments went to those who had voted against him.

Shirley was assigned to the Education Committee. She was delighted with the committee assignment, which matched her interests and experience.

Important work is done in legislative committees. It is in committees that bills are first introduced. Committee members study the bills and get them ready to present to the full body of

New York State Assembly in a night session.

legislators, who can vote them into law. Some bills never get out of committees. Assemblywoman Chisholm proposed significant pieces of legislation which directly affected people in her district. They also helped poor, disadvantaged people in other areas of the state. One of Shirley's bills created the SEEK program (Search for Education, Elevation, and Knowledge). It granted scholarships to minority students. The program recognized that not every bright high-school student was prepared for college work. Particularly in urban areas, high schools that enrolled large members of minority students did not offer college preparation. Not many of them had parents who could offer their children the support they needed as students. They did not advise them to take difficult courses or to ask teachers for help. Few poor parents had gone to college themselves. Although they wanted the best for their children, they didn't always know how to get it for them.

Shirley remembered the small number of black students who had attended Brooklyn College with her. She knew that many more could have been there if they had had parents like hers. Or if they had been able to attend Girls' High School. The students she wanted to help were bright enough to earn college degrees. But first they would need to learn the skills they had missed in high school. They would also need guidance from counselors who could take on the role of encouraging parents. These students needed to know that what they wanted was possible. They needed encouragement to study and to keep trying.

Financial help was also essential. With so much to make up, it was unrealistic to expect them to work while they were attending school. Yet most of them would be unable to attend college without some kind of income, because their families couldn't help. In some cases families would suffer without the income that they had counted on from these young people. Shirley was rewarded when in 1965 the SEEK bill was passed by the Assembly and Senate and became a law.

The next piece of legislation that she sponsored helped domestic workers. Shirley knew from her own mother's experience that there was little job protection for women who provided household help. Employers could let them go, suddenly cutting off their income. Usually, they weren't able to find another job right away. Shirley's bill required every employer who paid a household worker more than $500 a year to contribute to unemployment insurance. Employees who were covered by the insurance were able to collect benefits if they were laid off after her bill was voted into law in 1965.

In her first year, she was also successful in correcting an injustice against female schoolteachers. When they became pregnant and took maternity and child-care leaves, they lost their tenure rights. That meant that when they returned to work, they were considered beginners once again. Shirley's bill, which became a law in 1965, maintained their tenure and credit for experience.

Shirley shepherded other bills through the Education Committee. One raised the maximum amount of money that local school districts could spend on their students. The second bill provided state aid to day-care centers.

She voted against spending public money on textbooks for church-run schools. Shirley believed that such help violated the United States Constitution. She saw it as aid to religion, which the Constitution forbids. Despite opposition, the bill became law.

Once the legislative session began, she developed a routine that she would follow during her four-year service as an assemblywoman. From Monday to Thursday she stayed in Albany, attending meetings in the legislative building. In the evening, she carried legislation back with her to the hotel. While eating dinner alone in her room, she studied the legislation. Wanting to understand what she was voting for, she read everything about the new bills. After taking time to make up her mind, she rarely changed it. Before debates, she gathered the background information and studied the opposite side's arguments and personalities. She knew her facts and spoke easily and confidently.

Late Thursday she would take the train home to New York City, where she and Conrad shared the news of their week apart. On Friday evening, people who lived in the district came to see her at the Unity headquarters. Meeting with them one by one or in small groups in the back room of the district office, she listened to their problems. Unlike the old clubhouse arrangement where the leaders sat on a raised platform, Shirley and the other Unity leaders sat with the voters. The voters were considered equal partners in solving district problems.

The redistricting that occurred in 1964 was not final. Instead of having her seat for two years, Shirley had to run for it again at the end of her first session in Albany. A primary race in June 1965 and the general election the following November assured her place in the Assembly for the 1966 session. Her term ended with the conclusion of the 1966 legislative session. Then once again the lines were redrawn. She had to run in the 1966 primary and general elections to regain her seat for the 1967 session. In both general elections the Liberal Party also nominated her. That put her name on two ballots, the Democratic and the Liberal. She won each election with big margins. Her reputation as a proven vote-getter made it difficult for the party to ignore her next bid.

8

Congressional Bid

In 1967, Shirley Chisholm had her eye on Congress. Members of the House of Representatives, the lower house of Congress, represent election districts in every state.

A new opportunity resulted from the Supreme Court's ruling on election districts. The court's 1964 decision had ruled that all election districts had to contain the same number of voters. It required districts to be made up of neighborhoods that were geographically close. To comply with the Supreme Court decision, a new congressional district was drawn in central Brooklyn, the Twelfth Congressional District. Bedford-Stuyvesant, with adjacent Brownsville and Crown Heights, combined with Flatbush to form the new congressional district, regular in size and shape.

Edna Kelly, who had represented the old district for many years, went with a small part that had been split off and combined with another. This left the way clear for a candidate from the new Twelfth Congressional District. A number of people were interested in the new seat, but Shirley was the first to announce herself as a candidate for the June 1968 primary election.

All of the proposed candidates had names familiar to the voters.

A citizens' committee, the Committee for a Negro Congressman from Brooklyn, was formed. Committee members interviewed the candidates to make a recommendation. As the only woman, Shirley thought her chances were slim. The county organization had promised to stay out of the preliminary selection process, but Shirley doubted that they would. She expected the county leaders to oppose her. In her tenure in the Assembly, she had been too independent and not enough of a team player. The county leaders owed her nothing. It wouldn't surprise her if they tried to stop her candidacy right at the start.

But she won the endorsement of the citizens' committee, despite her lack of ties to the party. Committee members were impressed with her independence. Although the county organization did not make an official endorsement, the local political clubs did get involved. Democrats in the four Assembly Districts in the new Twelfth Congressional District met and chose an official candidate to run in the primary.

City councilman and former state senator William C. Thompson was the district leaders' choice. The leaders' backing assured Thompson of regular party funds for his campaign. When black labor leader Dolly Robinson announced her candidacy, it became a three-way primary battle. Most people thought that Robinson and Chisholm would split the women's vote, giving Thompson the election.

Shirley's first task was to analyze the population of the new congressional district. Reading the names of voters in the election listings revealed some important facts. She discovered which ethnic groups clustered in each section of the district. Noticing the Hispanic names, she knew her ability to speak Spanish would be helpful. The Crown Heights section had many Jewish homeowners. Although there were actually more blacks living in the district, the majority of registered voters was white. Many blacks still did not believe their votes would make a difference and so hadn't registered to vote. Increasing black voter registration would be one of Shirley's priorities.

Perhaps the most surprising statistic was the number of women in the district. They outnumbered men by thousands. Shirley knew that she would make a direct appeal for help to the women. The Unity Club workers scheduled dozens of small, living-room gatherings. There Shirley could meet the women in their own neighborhoods and they formed a solid block of support.

She had another surprise as she began her campaign, a phone call from Wesley McD. Holder. Her old political ally, whose friendship she had lost in the fight for the BSPL presidency, now offered his help. Mac had earlier realized his dream of seeing a black judge in Brooklyn. Now he wanted a black representative in Congress. Harlem had Adam Clayton Powell, Jr., and it was time for Brooklyn to have a black in Congress, too. Mac was convinced that Shirley was the best person to make that breakthrough. If he organized her campaign, he believed, she'd do it.

Together Shirley and Mac, with Unity backing, set to work. Unlike Thompson, who got his campaign funds from the regular Democrats, they had no money. Chisholm had to rely on small contributions from individuals to pay campaign expenses. But what the Unity Democrats lacked in money, they made up for in energy.

While the regular party candidate held organized meetings arranged by campaign workers, Shirley went to the streets. Beginning in February, she campaigned on her days off from the State Legislature. Wherever a small gathering was likely, she was ready to speak. She turned up on corners at busy intersections, in shopping centers, in parks. Her strength, she knew, was her four-year record as an assemblywoman.

She told the crowds about what she'd accomplished in the New York State Assembly. Capitalizing on her independence from the regular party organization, she adopted a slogan. VOTE FOR CHISHOLM FOR CONGRESS—UNBOUGHT AND UN-BOSSED, proclaimed her campaign literature. Volunteers in fleets of twenty to fifty cars drove through the district on weekends. The ten large housing projects in the district were regular stops on the campaign trail. Shirley shook hands with everyone who appeared. She talked and listened while workers distributed Chisholm shopping bags. In the bags were copies of a brief biography and other campaign literature. With Mac guiding her, Shirley delivered her message directly to the people. It was a message of hope. She

Shirley Chisholm aggressively campaigned for Congress against James Farmer and countered his image of her as a "little schoolteacher."

promised to represent all of the people in her district, but she made a special appeal to blacks to register to vote.

People listened to Shirley Chisholm. They listened to the clear voice that spoke to them of hope and belief in America. She called for an America of change in which they would become equal partners. The voice of hope never faltered although it was severely tested in April 1968. The assassination of Dr. Martin Luther King, Jr. was a hammer blow of tragedy. King's death caused an explosion of anger and fear in all Americans, but particularly in blacks. Dr. King had taught blacks pride and courage. He had made equality more than a dream—made it something to strive for.

Less than two months later, tragedy struck again. In early June 1968, Robert F. Kennedy was shot dead while campaigning for the Democratic presidential nomination. Senator Kennedy had worked closely with Bedford-Stuyvesant leaders to improve housing in the district and his loss was felt keenly there. Shirley mourned the deaths with the rest of the black community but urged people not to give in to despair. It was more important than ever that they work together constructively.

When the votes were counted in the June 18th primary, Shirley won by less than one thousand votes, a close margin. She had won the right to be the Democratic candidate for the Twelfth Congressional District race. Her next fight was in the general election.

Ordinarily, a Democratic nomination in Brooklyn assured victory in the general election. But the 1968 election became more complicated when the Liberal Party nominated James Farmer to oppose Shirley. The Republicans joined the Liberals and gave Farmer their nomination.

Farmer was a potentially strong candidate, even though he lived outside the district. The law did not require that a congressman live in the district he represented. The only requirement was that he reside in the state, and Farmer was a Manhattan resident, with an apartment near City Hall.

Nevertheless, James Farmer was as well known as if he did live in Brooklyn. As a former national director of CORE (Congress of Racial Equality), Farmer was a national figure. His face was familiar to TV viewers who had followed the freedom marches of the early 1960's. Farmer campaigned on his reputation as a tough advocate of civil rights. "Racists and bigots will be in strong positions in Congress. We need strong, experienced people who can command national attention to stand up to them. I don't intend to be a freshman in Congress. I graduated a long time ago," he said.

The Republican candidate took an apartment in Brooklyn when his campaign began. With his national reputation as a civil rights leader, Farmer attracted a great deal of the TV and print coverage of the campaign. No wonder the reporters and cameramen were mainly interested in Farmer. Some disregarded Shirley entirely.

Something was bothering Shirley. She didn't feel as well as she should. And it wasn't the excessively long days of campaigning. She'd always run strenuous campaigns and she had never felt this bad.

At Conrad's insistence she went to a doctor. Tests revealed a large tumor in her pelvis. Although the growth was not malignant, it had to be removed. Immediately.

Shirley protested. She could not understand why it was necessary to disrupt her campaign. The tumor had been growing for two years at least and was not cancerous. She pleaded with the doctor to wait until November to operate. But he insisted that he couldn't postpone the operation. Shirley went into Maimonides Hospital in late July 1968.

With the operation a success, she was up and walking the hospital corridors the next day, anxious to go home. Possibly because he knew she would go back to campaigning, the doctor kept her in the hospital.

Against his advice, Shirley immediately leapt back into the race. Seventeen pounds thinner than before the operation, and a little shaky, she had lost none of her fire. Before the stitches were out, she was back on her sound truck. Cruising through the district, she announced, "This is Fighting Shirley Chisholm, and I'm up and around in spite of what people are saying!"

To make up for lost time, Shirley and Mac opened a campaign office and dispatched a series of mailings. Taking an unpaid leave from his job, Mac developed a plan of attack against Farmer's campaign.

James Farmer emphasized the need for a "man's voice in Congress." His literature and speeches pounded home the strong male image. On his sound truck were young men with Afro haircuts wearing African-style, loose shirts called dashikis. They beat bongo drums as the truck rolled through the streets broadcasting Farmer's message. His brash and colorful campaign attracted TV broadcasters and newspaper reporters.

But Farmer's appeal to the men of the district backfired. He implicitly wanted the voters to choose him over his female opponent. What he hadn't noticed was the preponderance of women in the district. Ten thousand more women than men! But his analytically-minded foes had taken that figure seriously. Shirley and Mac had organized the women for Chisholm. Indignant with Farmer's hints of male superiority, the women threw themselves into the Chisholm campaign.

By late August, Shirley had still not regained her stamina. At the National Democratic Convention in Chicago, the New York delegation elected her their Democratic National Committeewoman. Shirley flew to Chicago to accept the post. But she was still not well enough to join the crowds in Convention Hall. Instead, she stayed in her hotel room and watched the convention news on TV.

The 1968 Democratic National Convention in Chicago was marked by protests against the war in Vietnam. Police efforts to curb the demonstrations ended in violence. Many Democrats worried that the terrible scenes outside the convention, viewed by millions on TV, would hurt their candidates in the November elections. The preceding spring had opened deep divisions in the party, with many candidates entered in primary races. Hubert Humphrey, chosen at the convention as Democratic presidential candidate, had a difficult job ahead. To gain a Democratic victory, he would have to unite the party.

Back home Shirley forced herself to take up the last phase of the campaign. The weeks between Labor Day in early September and Election Day are always the most intense time in a political campaign. As the official Democratic candidate in the Twelfth Congressional District, she now received help from the regular party organization. The organization scheduled her speeches and the number of volunteers grew. It was not necessary to spend as much time on street corners and in the housing projects as she did in the primary campaign.

She fiercely countered Farmer's male aggressiveness with her own fire. No one left a Shirley Chisholm address with Farmer's image of her as "the little schoolteacher." She attacked him as a carpetbagger, someone who comes into a district just to get elected to public office. Carpetbaggers usually do not have the best interest of their new home in mind. In fact they know little of its needs. Shirley played successfully on Farmer's unfamiliarity with Brooklyn. She knew Brooklyn and Brooklyn knew her.

Farmer and Chisholm agreed on the district's biggest concern: decentralized control of schools. Bedford-Stuyvesant residents wanted their own board of education to set policy for the schools. They wanted to make the decisions that a central, city-wide board was at present making for its children.

More than that, they agreed on the community's employment, housing, and health-care needs. Essentially, then, the voters had a choice between two candidates with similar views on important issues. They could vote for a strong and dedicated civil rights leader

Shirley Chisholm smilingly gives the "V" for victory sign after defeating civil rights leader James Farmer to become the first black congresswoman.

with a national reputation and political ambitions who had yet to be elected to public office. Or they could elect a homegrown candidate with roots in the community and a solid legislative record.

As a Republican, Farmer's national reputation could not overcome the disadvantage of a voting population that was 80 percent Democrat. In the end, his attempts to capture Brooklyn from the lady who had known its streets and gathering places since childhood failed. Chisholm won with better than a 2-1/2-to-1 victory.

When the votes were counted on the night of November 5, 1968, Chisholm's campaign workers at their second-floor headquarters broke into cheers. A petite figure in a light green knit suit, Shirley stood between her husband, Conrad, and Mac to accept a bouquet of chrysanthemums. Someone in the crowd yelled, "Let's go get Farmer and show him the way home." But Shirley was looking forward, not backward. "I know that as a freshman in Congress, I'm supposed to be seen and not heard," she said. "But my voice will be heard. I have no intention of being quiet," she promised.

With her election Brooklyn blacks were represented at every legislative level from City Council to Congress. Congresswoman-elect Shirley Chisholm, with Mac's help, was headed for Washington. Congress was about to welcome its first black female member.

9

The First Black Congresswoman

Shirley's victory caused a sensation. The broadcasters and reporters who had passed her by during the campaign were now anxious for interviews. As the newly elected Congresswoman from New York's Twelfth Congressional District, she was the first black woman to win a seat in the House of Representatives of the United States Congress. She was suddenly plunged into the excitement of being a celebrity. Conrad knew they would have to get away if they were to have any peace. They made their escape to the island of Jamaica for a vacation. Shirley was at last following her surgeon's orders and taking a long-delayed rest.

But three weeks later, she was anxious to get home. Once back in the U.S., she hurried to catch up with her preparations. She went straight to Washington to assemble an office staff in time for January, when the new Congress would meet. Members of Congress often reward campaign workers with staff jobs. But Shirley looked instead for the most competent and experienced people to staff her office. And she assigned women to every level of responsibility, not just to the lower-level jobs that they held in other congressional offices. Many, but not all, were black. Militant blacks urged her to assemble an all-black staff. But ability and loyalty were more important to Shirley than skin color.

Her office staff organized, she looked forward to taking her place in the new Congress. Although the new President, Richard M. Nixon, was a Republican, Democrats still had a majority of members in the House of Representatives and the Senate. Shirley hoped that the Congress and President could work together. They needed to heal the wounds of 1968. The country needed to go forward after the assassinations of Martin Luther King, Jr. and Robert F. Kennedy. The rage against the Vietnam War that crystallized at the Democratic National Convention would only end when the war ended, she knew. Nixon's pledge to terminate the war was a hopeful beginning.

The Ninety-first Congress began with a rap of Speaker John McCormack's gavel. On its rolls were nine black members, three of them new—the largest number of blacks ever to serve in the House of Representatives. The previous record was the Reconstruction Congress of 1873-74 after the Civil War, in which seven black representatives served. Shirley Chisholm was the only woman in the group.

The committee system of the United States Congress was similar to that of the New York State Assembly. A bill began in a committee where it was debated. If the committee members supported the bill, it would be brought to the full legislative body. The Congress would then study it further. At some point, a vote would be taken. If passed by both houses of Congress, the House of Representatives and the Senate, the bill would then go to the president. His signature was the final step in the process of turning a bill into a law. If the president disapproved of the bill, he could send it back to Congress. There it could be abandoned, modified, or reaffirmed without change, and sent back to the president.

Committee members are powerful because their decisions determine the fate of bills, many of which never get out of committees and onto the House floor. When Shirley went to the New York Assembly, she was happy with her committee assignment. As a member of the Education Committee, she had brought her own knowledge and background to the decisions she was asked to make. She knew that it would be difficult to get such a good assignment in the House of Representatives. There were more representatives in the United States Congress than in the New York State Assembly and many had been House members for a very long time.

Committee seats were assigned by the seniority system. Those representatives who had been in Congress the longest were assigned to the committees they chose. Many seats had been held for years by the same people. Chairman of the House Ways and Means Committee Wilbur Mills made all the assignments. Newcomers had to wait years to get on the committee of their choice.

Still, Shirley believed that her knowledge of the cities and her experience as an educator would weigh in her assignment. People with whom she discussed the issue did not encourage her. The Education and Labor Committee was a much sought-after assignment. Nevertheless, Shirley kept hoping. She knew that the committee had several vacant Democratic seats. But if she didn't get the Education and Labor assignment, she would be satisfied with the Banking and Currency Committee, which had control of housing construction, a critical issue in her district.

Shirley contacted a Democrat on the Education Committee whom she knew from New York. He agreed to speak on her behalf. She also sent a copy of her résumé to every Democratic member of the Ways and Means Committee. She was convinced that they would be impressed with her experience.

Even after the many warnings she'd had about the seniority system, she was horrified when word leaked out that the House Ways and Means Committee had assigned her to the House Agriculture Committee. It certainly was not her choice, although it did control food stamps and migrant workers. However, her subcommittee assignment was to forestry and rural development. That was intolerable!

"Apparently all they know here in Washington about Brooklyn is that a tree grew there," Shirley stormed, referring to the famous book, *A Tree Grows in Brooklyn*.

She had no knowledge or experience to bring to the forestry subcommittee. Moreover, she had gone to Washington to help solve the problems of her own district and that of other inner cities. She wanted to make life better for her constituents, the people in Brooklyn whom she represented and people like them who lived in other urban areas. She knew that she had to ask for another assignment.

More experienced legislators told her that it couldn't be done. No one asks for a change, they told her. Everyone just had to accept the assignment they'd been given. In time, people told her, she would work her way up to the committee she wanted.

But Shirley believed the seniority system was unfair. Only members of Congress who had served many years had access to the best committees. Yet it was newly elected representatives who often had the freshest ideas. She had spent the summer in close contact with the people who had elected her. Aware of their needs, she had come to Congress determined to help them. Accepting the Agricultural Committee placement would completely rule that out. She decided to bring her problem to the Speaker of the House of Representatives, John McCormack of Massachusetts. McCormack was in his eighties and a veteran of many years as a congressman. Her first meeting with him had been at the swearing-in ceremony for new members on the first day of the session. Later that same day at her hotel, McCormack had repeated the ceremony for relatives and friends who were unable to get into the gallery.

"I don't know if this is protocol, Mr. Speaker," she said, "but I wanted to talk to you because I feel my committee and subcommittee assignment do not make much sense."

"Mrs. Chisholm, this is the way it is," he said. "You have to be a good soldier."

Shirley thought about the streets in her district lined with gray tenements. She saw again the blank stares of unemployed men sitting on the stoops, ground down from years of poverty. "The time is growing late, and I can't be a good soldier any longer," she answered. "It does not make sense to put a black woman representative on a subcommittee dealing with forestry. I will do what I have to do, regardless of the consequences."

Troubled by her insistence, McCormack agreed to speak to Wilbur Mills. No change was made, however.

Shirley knew that a closed caucus, or meeting, of Democratic House members had to agree to committee assignments. She decided that this was the forum in which she would make her objection public.

In the caucus, she learned that the senior member standing was the first one recognized. Each time she rose to ask her question, more experienced congressmen were recognized. Wilbur Mills was in the Speaker's chair, and she wondered if he was deliberately passing over her. Or were the other congressmen preventing her from being recognized? She wasn't sure. Finally she walked up to the space directly below the Speaker's chair where everyone could see her. After recognizing several more people, Mills at last asked why she was standing there.

"I would just like to tell the caucus why I vehemently reject my committee assignment." Over the buzz that greeted her statement, she went on to deliver her prepared remarks. She cited her twenty years' experience in education and her work on behalf of education in the New York State Assembly. She reminded the chairman of the small number of black congressmen and suggested a way to correct the imbalance. If the black representatives were placed in key committee positions, they could exert proportionately more influence.

Later Shirley was invited to submit a resolution removing her name from the Agriculture Committee. At the end of the day, representatives approached her, warning that she had "committed political suicide." Shirley chuckled at the familiar phrase.

Shirley did receive a new committee assignment, to the Veterans' Affairs Committee. Although it was not one of her choices, it was better than Agriculture. As she told friends, "There are a lot more veterans in my district than there are trees."

With her committee assignment out of the way, Shirley had time to set some goals. Her first priority was to help people from her district resolve individual problems. Because only nine of the 435 House members were black, she knew that she also had to be an advocate for people outside her district who did not feel represented. In particular, black and minority residents of the District of Columbia sought her help. With no voting representative of their own in Congress, they turned to her as if she were their congresswoman.

Her second goal was to use the legislative process for programs that promoted equality. She hoped to support housing and education aid to the cities. Existing laws that would end discrimination in federally funded jobs had to be upheld. Shirley believed that new laws to end discrimination were needed less than a commitment to obey and enforce existing laws.

Women's groups that wanted to extend abortion rights saw Shirley Chisholm as their special advocate. Women's groups wanted to extend abortion rights to all women by repealing laws that made abortion illegal. As a New York State assemblywoman, Shirley had supported bills that would have made it easier for women whose lives were endangered to have abortions. But she had not been in favor of removing all restrictions on abortions.

Those who objected to abortion said that it was murder to take the life of an unborn child. That was why many church groups opposed abortion. Many black people were suspicious of the abortion movement, seeing it as an attempt to limit the numbers of black babies born. These opposition groups wanted to maintain the laws that made abortion illegal.

Others recognized that women were having abortions anyway but having them illegally. Middle-class women could find doctors who knew how to get around the law. But the poor either resorted to unskilled doctors or tried to perform the abortions themselves. Women's groups urged Shirley to state her position on the issue of abortion law repeal. She listened to both sides of the argument. In

Shirley Chisholm greeting students on the steps of the United States Capitol in the 1960's.

September 1968, she was asked to become president of the newly formed National Association for the Repeal of Abortion Laws. By then she had researched the abortion issue, searched her own conscience, and taken a position on the issue. Although she had to decline the office because of her commitments to Congress, she accepted the position of honorary president. In that capacity, she lent her name to the movement and pledged her support to repeal legislation. She also continued to work for a full range of family planning services that was not based on ability to pay. She favored safe, effective family planning methods.

Her stand on the abortion issue baffled her colleagues in the House of Representatives who knew that it was politically unwise. Few members of Congress had taken a stand on either side of the controversial issue. Abortion was too hot to touch. Knowing that only a groundswell of support would bring abortion legislation to a vote, Shirley abandoned it until a more favorable climate developed.

The year of Shirley Chisholm's arrival in Congress was also a mayoral election year in New York City. Incumbent Republican Mayor John V. Lindsay was not nominated for reelection by his party. Undeterred, Lindsay decided to run as the Liberal Party candidate. Opposing him was the official Republican candidate, John Marchi, and Mario A. Procaccino, the Democrat. Both of the major party candidates wanted to combat social change by returning things to the way they used to be. Neither seemed sympathetic to the needs of the poor and the minorities.

As one of the two New York State National Democratic Committee members, Shirley Chisholm was expected to support Democratic candidates. In 1969 that meant campaigning for Procaccino, and Shirley knew that she couldn't possibly do it. Some politicians with her dilemma would avoid calling attention to their feelings. They might vacation or schedule a legislative research trip out of the country. Both Shirley's husband, Conrad, and her close political ally, Mac, advised her against announcing support for Lindsay. The Democrats' anger would affect her for years to come. But Shirley sincerely believed that Lindsay's views were closer to hers and the people she represented. She believed, therefore, that he deserved her active support. Her TV appearance at a Lindsay press conference broadcast from Gracie Mansion, the mayor's residence, shocked the New York Democratic Party. Procaccino and the Democrats in counties outside the city called for her ouster from the Democratic National Committee.

But Shirley stuck to her position. She reminded the Democrats that the great Democratic president, Franklin Delano Roosevelt, had supported a Republican New York mayor, Fiorello La Guardia. She affirmed herself as a leader who had to stand up for the people she represented. She campaigned for Lindsay and was not removed from her committee seat. Lindsay won the election.

When Shirley Chisholm came to Washington in 1969, the war in Vietnam had raged for more than seven years. TV coverage of Americans fighting in the jungles of southeast Asia came into American homes every evening on the news. During President Lyndon Johnson's administration, from 1963 to 1968, the war had escalated. Thousands of American soldiers and billions of dollars had been committed to the struggle. Johnson had increased America's participation, hoping to bring the war to an end. But the end was still not in sight during his last year in office.

The stalemate took an enormous toll in American lives lost in action. At home, student outrage had led to the rioting between demonstrators and the Chicago police outside the Democratic National Convention in 1968. Some said later that the rioting and the police response had cost the Democrats the election. Many other confrontations took place between law enforcement officials and young people. All over the country, students were protesting the war. "Hell, no! We won't go!" they shouted as they marched and demonstrated.

In the early days of the new administration, hopes were high about bringing the war to an end. Everyone awaited the Nixon plan promised during the presidential campaign. But time was passing and still the war raged. Its costs were interfering with other programs. In March the Secretary of Health, Education, and Welfare warned that money for needed hospitals and schools was not available.

On a single day when she heard two separate announcements from the president, Shirley Chisholm lost hope that the Nixon

President Richard M. Nixon conducting a press conference.

administration would keep its promise. On that day, President Nixon said that the nation's defense system would not be secure until an antiballistic missile system (ABM) was built. He intended to push for its development. The ABM program would cost billions of dollars and be a huge investment of time and priorities. The second announcement warned of a cutback in the District of Columbia's Head Start program, which gave needy children pre-school experience. The program was out of funds.

In her first speech to the House, Shirley linked the two announcements. She believed that they were symbolic of the way priorities were determined in government. Social and educational programs were historically sacrificed to military needs. Shirley expressed her intention of voting against bills that provided military support, until every American had adequate shelter, food and education. Pacifism was not her message. She believed firmly in defending her country. It was the conduct of the war that offended her. Money was committed to a war thousands of miles across the Pacific Ocean. Yet funds were scarce for the cold, hungry, and illiterate in the USA.

"Our children, our jobless men, our deprived, rejected and starving fellows, our dejected citizens must come first," she declared. "For this reason I intend to vote 'no' on every money bill that comes to the floor of this House that provides funds for the Department of Defense."

Many of Shirley's colleagues misunderstood, thinking that she was abandoning the servicemen. But young people understood. They knew that her objective was exactly the opposite, to bring American troops home. On campuses across the nation, they knew that Shirley Chisholm was taking a stand for them in Washington.

10

Will She Run?

While Congress was in session, Shirley lived in a rented, Washington apartment from Sunday night until Thursday evening. Although very like the routine she had followed as an assemblywoman in Albany, life as a member of the U.S. House of Representatives was more demanding. Congress continued to meet long past April, the usual end of the State Assembly sessions. And there was a great deal more information to absorb. She had to become familiar with the special needs of people in different parts of the country and with a whole range of issues affecting them.

Almost immediately after Shirley's first election to Congress in 1968, letters from students began to arrive. The letters expressed support for her stand on ending the Vietnam War and many included requests for her to speak on campuses. But she knew that she would have to decline all but a very few invitations. As a new member of the House of Representatives, she was still learning to be an effective congresswoman, and that was her first priority.

But she found the students hard to refuse. Office staff members had to help her choose carefully from the hundreds of requests that arrived each week. Even though she declined most of the invitations. she delivered more speeches than any other member of the House of Representatives. By the end of her second term, in 1972, she had spoken on more than one hundred campuses.

Shirley knew that many young people had turned away from politics after the terrible events of 1968. She remembered the idealistic students who had worked for Eugene McCarthy early in his primary campaign for the Democratic presidential nomination in 1968. McCarthy's speeches against the Vietnam War attracted them. Many students had left their college campuses to follow him on his lonely trip to the first important primary fight in New Hampshire. Their support was solid evidence of mounting resistance to the war. They had stayed through his early primary victories. Later, others had campaigned for Robert F. Kennedy when he also became a presidential candidate. These young people were passionate in their demand that America's leaders look both backward and forward. A backward look to recall the idealistic principles of the country's beginnings; forward to extend those principles to all Americans.

Shirley continued her resistance to the war in Vietnam and made it part of her 1970 campaign for a second term. Easily regaining her congressional seat, she prepared more carefully for an Education and Labor Committee assignment. This time she followed the rules and promised her support to fellow representatives who were seeking committee chairmanships. She hoped that they would use their influence with the Ways and Means Committee and get her the prized assignment. Her strategy worked. Shirley was seated on the Education and Labor Committee at the beginning of her second term in January 1971.

The second year of Shirley's second term, 1972, was a presidential election year. Democrats were determined not to repeat the mistakes of four years earlier, when students and other anti-war protesters tried to get into the Democratic National Convention.

Young people, both black and white, welcomed Shirley

92

wherever she went. From the beginning of her appearances on college campuses, they always asked about her plans for 1972. They had no faith in the Nixon-Agnew team and they wanted a change. Would she think of running for president, they wondered.

In response, she repeated the statement that she'd made long ago to Professor Warsoff at Brooklyn College. Remember, she pointed out, that she was black and a woman. But as the question recurred, even she began to doubt her position. Perhaps she *should* think about entering the presidential race as a candidate. Perhaps the double handicap could be overcome. After all, though a black woman, she had been elected to Congress!

Shirley was convinced that the increasing numbers of blacks serving in elective office should have a significant effect on the election. She believed that it would be impossible to take black voters for granted again. The voter-registration campaigns of the early 60's had changed the patterns of many election districts. In the northern cities of Cleveland, Ohio and Gary, Indiana, black mayors governed. Other blacks held important posts in federal, state, and city governments. By 1971, there were thirteen black members of the House of Representatives. They began to meet as a group and called themselves the Black Congressional Caucus. Their faces were familiar to newspaper readers and TV viewers. Familiar too were leaders of black organizations, such as Roy Innis of the National Association for the Advancement of Colored People and the Reverend Jesse Jackson of Operation Breadbasket, a self-help program.

But perhaps no face was as familiar as Shirley Chisholm's. She was as well known as any of the announced candidates. The first black congresswoman, she had been pursued by the news media since coming to Congress almost four years earlier. Her strong statements on the war and domestic problems were widely publicized. In big cities and small towns, she was mentioned as a potential candidate.

Shirley herself wondered if she should enter the primary races, the first step to nomination. As a candidate, she could discuss the problems facing the country and offer solutions to those problems. In July 1971, following her own instincts and the suggestions of many in her audiences, she began to drop hints about being a candidate. She hoped to discover what kind of real support she could expect.

Other black leaders were determined to exert influence on the presidential elections of November 1972. But to do so they needed a plan of attack. They represented many different groups of voters. Most black leaders were from big, densely populated cities. But they were from different regions of the country and did not always agree. Julian Bond, a Georgia state legislator, represented a largely rural state. Georgians had different needs from the voters who elected Percy Sutton, a borough president in New York City.

In the fall of 1971, a group of important black leaders held a series of meetings in Chicago. In the group were mayors and congressmen from urban areas, labor leaders, and officials of black organizations. The section of the city where the meetings took place, Northlake, gave its name to the gatherings.

Shirley was invited but she did not attend. At the time she had still not received any encouragement from the black leaders. Not even the Black Caucus in Congress, of which she was a member, had shown any interest.

She was convinced that she would distract the black leaders if she attended the Northlake meetings. Her presence, she believed, would prevent them from drafting a plan of action, their first and most important task. But if she attended, they might not get to that first step at all. Instead, they would focus on Shirley Chisholm, who was sounding more like a candidate every day. Therefore she sent one of her young aides, Thaddeus Garrett, in her place. Garrett wanted her to run for president. He reported back to her on the plans

Congresswoman Shirley Chisholm with the United States Capitol in the background.

discussed at Northlake, all designed to gain control of delegates to the 1972 Democratic National Convention.

Delegates' votes at the convention determine the party's candidates. Convention delegates also help decide which programs the candidates will support, if elected. Voters choose delegates who support their candidates or their issues.

Selecting delegates for conventions begins with primary elections in the states. These are held early in the year, before the conventions. In the primary elections voters choose delegates to attend the convention and vote for one of the presidential candidates. Some delegates run in the primaries already pledged to a particular candidate. Other delegates are uncommitted at that time.

The men at Northlake discussed the merits of different strategies to attract delegates. Manhattan Borough President Percy Sutton suggested a simple, direct strategy. He urged the black leaders to agree on a single minority candidate to run for the party's nomination. They should play to win by pooling resources, he argued, to commit the maximum number of delegates to the minority candidate. Sutton's strategy would challenge the majority candidates, and offer the voters a new face, a new voice, and a new message.

The men of Northlake couldn't agree on a plan. When Shirley was proposed as the candidate, the group rejected her. Its members, who were all black men, were not ready to support a woman. They claimed that she would be the women's candidate, not the blacks'. Thaddeus Garrett disagreed. "She is a black woman, of the black experience, and from one of the blackest districts in the country," he argued. "She can do nothing but be black in her dealings."

Both Garrett and Representative Ronald Dellums of California believed that she was the perfect coalition candidate. They knew that she could attract black and white poor, young people, and the elderly. "She could have a dramatic effect on politics in this country," Dellums told the press. "She could bring together the elements necessary to create a third force in American politics."

The Northlake meetings were a disappointment to Shirley Chisholm and other black leaders. No coalition was formed, nor was a plan drafted. Some of the Northlake men left the meetings intending to support one of the major candidates. Others planned to stay with local candidates, or "favorite sons," in the primary elections.

Shirley was more than ever convinced that the time had come for a black candidate. The men who had attended the Northlake meetings all possessed leadership qualities, she knew. Any one of them could have been an acceptable black candidate of the Democratic Party for president of the United States. But that was the problem; a black candidate was self-limiting.

A candidate was needed who would speak for *all* who could not speak for themselves. Such a candidate would represent blacks and other minorities, youth, women, the poor, and the elderly. They needed someone who was a genuine contrast to the usual party choice.

None of the men at Northlake were under real pressure to run. On the other hand, "Chisholm for President" volunteers were begging to begin. Once she gave the word to set up local and state campaign organizations, they'd be ready. Not only women and blacks, but Spanish-speaking voters and college students of all races were urging her to run.

Shirley's mail made it clear that she had become an advocate for minorities in every part of the country. But she still wondered how much real support she'd have if she ran for the Democratic nomination. A political campaign needs people, lots of them. Would the college students and the women join forces with her? Would there be enough workers to attend to the hundreds of details of a campaign? She worried about going into debt. Running for a party nomination cost hundreds of thousands of dollars.

Only a small number of black politicians encouraged Shirley's hints about running. Angry and impatient, she addressed the issue in a speech at a Black exposition in Chicago. Organized by the Reverend Jesse Jackson and his Operation Breadbasket, the exposition highlighted black achievement in the arts, social programs, and business. Shirley spoke at a workshop on women in politics. In the strongest terms, she told her audience that she had felt more resistance because she was a woman than because she was a black.

The lukewarm support did not stop her, however. She told a reporter that day, "The endorsements I have so far come from those who are not regarded as leaders. . . . My backing is from just plain people, and this is enough for me. That will be my inspiration, if I do make the decision to accept the challenge."

But she needed money as well as words. A professional campaign manager, office expenses, staff in many parts of the country, campaign literature and printing costs, radio and TV time for paid political announcements all cost money. Shirley and Conrad were not wealthy. Nor were their friends. She needed contributions from people who thought she would make a good president.

Large contributions to a Chisholm campaign were unlikely, she knew. She couldn't run a full-scale campaign in all fifty states. Campaigning would have to be limited to states that might give her delegates and skip the states where other candidates were strong.

In Brooklyn, she had made up for her lack of funds with will and energy. Personal contacts in the streets and downtown areas had drawn votes there, but she knew there was no way to translate that direct experience to a national campaign. What Shirley Chisholm needed was money and lots of it!

Candidates who scored high in the early primaries attracted attention. With attention came campaign contributions. Two states, New Hampshire and Florida, had early primaries, both in March. Without enough money to enter even one primary, Shirley couldn't consider entering two at the same time.

She decided to pass up New Hampshire and concentrate on Florida, with its significant number of black voters. If she received 5 or 6% of the Florida vote, people might consider her a serious candidate and contribute money. The warm reception to her Miami Beach speech in July 1971, with its first hint about running, was a good start. And one of Shirley's strongest supporters, Gwendolyn Cherry, was a representative in the Florida legislature.

Cherry invited her to the Orange Bowl in December. On her weekend visit, Shirley met people who urged her to run in the Florida primary. She'd need their help, she told them. They would have to start a campaign fund. Their promises of support and favorable newspaper publicity helped make up her mind.

Shirley made two tours in Florida, the first early in January and the second after her announcement to run. On the first tour she drove home the urgent need for funds. At a men's luncheon club in Miami and a Democratic Women's Club meeting in Tampa, she reached people who could contribute to her campaign. She appeared at press conferences and fund-raisers ranging from box suppers to banquets. But she didn't forget the students. College auditoriums were free and students were anxious to hear Shirley. At the University of Florida and at Florida A. & M., they turned out in record numbers. In mock elections, called straw polls, Florida students ranked her second.

The first tour was a whirlwind, tossing her across the state from Pensacola to Jacksonville, from Fort Lauderdale to St. Petersburg. The trip ended with a motorcade in Jacksonville, with another round of meetings and fund raisers. She spoke there to the National Organization of Women and the League of Women Voters, and was interviewed on TV. Shirley came back to Washington from the first Florida trip excited about the spirit she had kindled.

On January 25, 1972, she called a press conference at Brooklyn's largest Baptist church. Surrounded by her husband Conrad Chisholm, Wesley McDonald Holder, the Unity office staff, and as many Brooklyn supporters as could squeeze into the crowded church, Shirley faced the TV cameras and reporters.

"I stand before you today as a candidate for the Democratic Party nomination for the Presidency of the United States. I am the candidate of the people," she said.

The most stylish hat of the 1972 presidential campaign was officially in the ring.

11

The Democratic Presidential Primary Campaign

Shirley Chisholm returned to Florida on March 8th as an announced candidate for the Democratic National Party nomination for president of the United States. Before she left New York City, Manhattan borough president Percy Sutton endorsed her. Sutton was well known in Florida and she knew the endorsement would help. This second trip was a campaign to win delegates in Florida's March 14th primary.

As expected, Chisholm-for-President contributions increased after her announcement. But donations were small and not nearly enough for a full-scale campaign. From the beginning it was clear that Shirley Chisholm would not have the same generous financial backing as the other candidates. She started with $44,000, far from the minimum of $300,000 that she would need. Lack of money forced her to rely on volunteers to organize the Florida campaign. She was counting on a successful finish in the Florida primary to attract additional funds.

Wherever Shirley drew a crowd, she received an enthusiastic response. Although she had presented herself as a candidate of all the people, she made a special appeal to blacks. As the first national black candidate for a major-party nomination, she pleaded for their support.

Together, she told them, they could convince Democratic leaders to look beyond white male leadership. "We can turn things around if we put it together," she told one group. "I am your instrument for change. . . . give your votes to me instead of one of those warmed-over gentlemen who come to you once every four years. Give your vote to me. I belong to you."

She hoped that a strong showing on her part would increase the role of minorities. She wanted to put a black on the ticket, a woman in charge of the Department of Health, Education and Welfare, and an Indian at the head of the Department of Interior.

Along with the emotional highs of the Florida swing came problems. These same problems would plague Shirley's whole campaign for the presidential nomination. The professional manager whom she hired quit in frustration before the Florida primary. Without a paid staff, he had been unable to organize the volunteers who came from many different factions. Each faction wanted to operate independently. Women's groups and black organizations were jealous of one another. Instead of working together, they competed. As a result, her appearances were sometimes inaccurately announced or not publicized at all. With different people scheduling her speeches, there were conflicts and confusion about where she would appear. Without funds for paid publicity, her volunteers had to rely on free notices in church bulletins and telephone calls to newspapers and TV stations. Not a single poster or announcement heralded her University of Miami appearance. Last minute word-of-mouth news drew only a small group of students.

Still, Shirley knew that she had no other options. Without the hefty treasuries of the major candidates, she had to rely on her hardworking and dedicated volunteers. She reminded Conrad of her first Assembly and Congressional races that she had won against heavy odds. People power had overcome in Brooklyn; perhaps it could in Florida too—and ultimately in the nation.

The Florida primary field drew many other Democratic candidates. They were anxious to demonstrate their popularity in the South with a strong early showing, because the Democratic Party needed a candidate who could win the Southern vote. If the South turned to the more conservative Republican Party, the Democrats would lose the general election.

Shirley, who had hoped to claim 5 or 6 % of the Florida primary vote, actually received just 4 percent. Some said that her late start was responsible for the modest showing. But another problem was lukewarm support from Florida's black political leaders, who really did not believe that the Chisholm campaign had a chance. Many of them had already committed to one of the major candidates. Hoping for help with their own reelection bids, they backed the candidate whom they thought might win. But 4 percent was tantalizingly close to what she'd hoped for, and Shirley decided to stay in the race.

In the following months, she took her campaign to New Jersey, Massachusetts, Minnesota, California, Michigan, and North Carolina. The trips to each state were brief, squeezed into the congressional schedule. With her new Education and Labor Committee seat, she wanted to be in the House of Representatives for important votes. Sometimes she had to cancel a campaign engagement at the last minute because of congressional responsibilities.

Cancellations disappointed volunteers who had arranged and promoted the events. Her Wisconsin state coordinator quit, convinced that he'd be more effective working for George McGovern. In spite of the fact that she didn't have the time or money to make a single appearance in Wisconsin, she won 9,100 votes in the primary. Results like that encouraged her to persevere.

In a three-day tour right before the April 25th Massachusetts primary, she concentrated on pro-Chisholm districts. The strategy earned her seven Massachusetts delegates.

After Massachusetts, Shirley Chisholm faced North Carolina, a state she had been warned to stay away from. Supporters of its local candidate or "favorite son," Terry Sanford, warned that she'd take votes from him. If that happened, George Wallace, the governor of Alabama, who was also running, might win the North Carolina primary.

Wallace, famous for his unswerving resistance to school integration, was popular in the South. The Sanford team spread the word: "A vote for Shirley Chisholm is a vote for George Wallace."

Shirley Chisholm in her Washington, D.C. office, with pre-schoolers, in the 1970's.

She attracted less than the 15% needed to win delegates in North Carolina and left the state with nothing for her efforts.

Next she headed for the Midwest. In Minnesota, Hubert H. Humphrey's home state, Shirley won eight delegates.

Well-organized women in Michigan planned a near-professional tour and a series of appearances. School desegregation was the big issue in Michigan. A recent court decision in that state had ordered busing to integrate white and black children in city public schools. Shirley supported busing only because it was a way to desegregate schools quickly. She knew that segregated housing was the real culprit. Blacks were not able to live in many parts of big cities. Until housing patterns were changed, children would have to be bused to achieve desegregation. In Kalamazoo, she addressed the issue of racism directly: "Traditionally, the Presidency has been the exclusive domain of a sole segment of our society—white males. This says to the others in our multifaceted, multiracial society that they unfortunately don't have the leadership or the brainpower to lead. This is no time to be hung up on sex or race. In 1972, we Americans need the best collective abilities of all our people. We Americans need to lift the burdens of unfairness and discrimination from the shoulders of so many of our fellow countrymen, of both sexes, all ages, and all races. . . . Who knows? It took a little black woman, Harriet Tubman, to lead three hundred of her people out of slavery. . . . it may take another little black woman 'to bring us together' in these troubled times of war and worry."

But the busing issue swung the Michigan primary on May 16th to George Wallace; despite Shirley's moving appeal, she came in behind Wallace, McGovern, and Humphrey.

Even before she learned these results, however, other disturbing news reached her: Governor George Wallace of Alabama had been shot. Shirley and her aides heard the first report on May 15th as they wound up their three-day tour of Michigan. Further details reached them at the airport before they left for California, the next primary state. Once again, hate and madness had provoked an attack on a public figure. Martin Luther King, Jr. and Robert F. Kennedy had been assassinated only four years earlier. Would 1972 be another year of tragedy and violence, like 1968?

Deeply disturbed by the shooting, Shirley visited George Wallace in the hospital. Although the two political leaders were far apart in their beliefs, she sympathized with Wallace as another human being. While he recovered in a hospital near Washington, D.C., she went with a staff member and a Secret Service agent to see him. She wanted him to know that despite their differences, she condemned the attempt on his life.

Many people were convinced that a political motive prompted her. The publicity surrounding the visit shocked Shirley. She was troubled that people did not recognize a simple act of kindness.

The Wallace shooting prompted special precautions. Upon her arrival in California on May 15, Shirley was assigned Secret Service protection. From then until the end of the Democratic National Convention in July, agents traveled with her.

Shirley's husband Conrad welcomed the Secret Service. He had taken a leave of absence from his job as an investigator for the City Bureau of Medical Service to travel with her. But still he worried about her safety, knowing that she was a perfect target. Despite letters expressing hatred that arrived regularly, and some threats, Shirley seemed fearless when she spoke before crowds. Afterward, people surrounded her, staying to ask questions or wish her well. The crowds were warm and supportive and she never turned them away. Until May 15, it was up to Conrad and her aides to protect her. But professional security was what she really needed, particularly after the attack on Wallace.

California was a primary that she hadn't wanted to enter. In this winner-take-all state, the candidate who received the most votes received all the delegates. But the Chisholm treasury could not afford the expensive campaign needed to gain first place in the California primary.

California, however, was the home state of Congressman Ronald V. Dellums, her earliest and strongest supporter in the Black Congressional Caucus. And the winner-take-all system had already been challenged. The Democratic National Convention would resolve the question in July. If the challenge to the system succeeded, more than one candidate would be able to gain California delegates.

In-fighting among rival Chisholm groups, a problem in Florida, recurred in California because no paid professional organization was possible. Black groups and women's groups went their separate ways instead of working together on Shirley's behalf. She came in third in the primary, with no delegates under the winner-take-all system. However, if the challenge to the system succeeded, she stood to gain twelve California delegates.

The Chisholm campaign ended with the California primary. Shirley had twenty-eight delegates, short of the fifty that she had hoped to bring to the convention. She now pinned her hopes on getting a share of the California delegates and on attracting uncommitted delegates at the convention in July.

Delegates to the 1972 Democratic Party National Convention started to gather in Miami Beach on Saturday, July 8th. Shirley was the last candidate to arrive. Landing at Miami International Airport in the early hours of Sunday morning, she was met by a group of Chisholm supporters, reporters and photographers. Secret Service agents whisked her, Conrad, and her two aides past the small crowd and into a waiting car. Surrounded by motorcycles and flashing red lights, they sped away. Another crowd waited at her headquarters hotel in Miami Beach. Waving Chisholm campaign signs, the men and women followed her into the lobby. Acknowledging their cheers, she thanked Mayor Kenneth Gibson, of Newark, New Jersey, who had come to welcome her.

Shirley's thoughts were racing ahead to the next day and she slept little that night. Black leaders had still not formed a bloc, or coalition, to give substance to their demands. Shirley hoped that she could rally them before the challenge to California's winner-take-all system was settled for good. Before the convention began, a partial ruling against the winner-take-all system had come from the Credentials Committee. McGovern, Humphrey, and Chisholm were thus each entitled to a share of the California votes. However, the ruling was not yet final, and the question still awaited a full convention vote.

At a meeting of the black caucus of the convention on Sunday, Shirley was the first of three candidates to speak. She challenged the caucus to take a daring step. She pleaded with its members to vote for her on the first ballot. If they couldn't do that, she urged them at least to remain uncommitted. McGovern might be persuaded to make pledges on black and minority issues if he sensed that a first ballot victory was still in doubt.

The next speaker was McGovern. He asked outright for support on keeping the winner-take-all system intact. He made no promises, but only reminded black delegates of his civil rights record.

The black caucus did not unite on Sunday as Shirley had hoped. On Monday night, the California challenge was rejected and McGovern received all of that state's delegates. When the challenge was settled, Muskie and Henry Jackson withdrew as candidates. In a surprise move, Hubert Humphrey released his black delegates to vote for Chisholm on the first ballot. Humphrey knew that he could not win a first-ballot victory and saw the release as symbolic. If no one else won and voting went to a second ballot, he would be back in the race, and would expect his delegates back. Humphrey's action was denounced as a "Stop McGovern" move.

But Thaddeus Garrett, Shirley's aide, gladly accepted ninety Humphrey delegates. Garrett hammered away at other uncommitted delegates and he continued to work on the black caucus of the convention. At the very last minute before balloting began, Garrett succeeded in getting the black caucus to endorse Chisholm. At that late hour, the caucus delegates realized what was happening. Too many people had already pledged themselves to McGovern or one of the other front runners. Those candidates had no need to bargain for voters. Black caucus members among the convention delegates hoped that they could still make a difference by uniting behind Shirley.

On Wednesday night, July 12th, 1972, Percy Sutton, borough president of Manhattan, mounted the Speaker's stand. He placed the name of Shirley Chisholm in nomination as a Democratic Party candidate for president of the United States. Charles Evers, Mayor of Fayette, Mississippi, seconded the nomination. In the frenzy of

Congresswoman Chisholm with members of the Black Congressional Caucus.

cheering, band playing, and noise making, Shirley Chisholm stepped to the lectern to accept the nomination. Dazzled by the flashbulbs, she watched her supporters wave banners and flags. The hubbub continued even when she began to speak.

An outsider, who did not know who the certain winner was, could easily have mistaken the fanfare for a victory celebration. But, at this peak moment, Shirley Chisholm had come to the end of her journey. Not the successful candidate, she had nevertheless won a unique victory. She had proved that a black and a woman could run for president of the United States. She was the first.

12

Professor Chisholm

After the nominations, balloting began. The states were called one by one, according to an order determined by lottery. On the first ballot, George McGovern's votes topped the 1,509 needed for nomination. The states that had not yet voted followed convention custom and cast all their votes for McGovern. Shirley Chisholm came in fourth, after McGovern, Wallace, and Henry Jackson, and ahead of North Carolina's Terry Sanford. Thaddeus Garrett was convinced that if the voting had gone to a second ballot, many more delegates would have switched to Chisholm. His efforts increased her votes to 152 on the first and only ballot.

When the convention ended, Shirley Chisholm returned to the House of Representatives to serve out the rest of her second term. In the fall of 1972, she was reelected to her House seat. McGovern, however, lost his presidential bid, and Richard M. Nixon began his second term as president in January 1973.

In the new Congress, Shirley continued to pursue her legislative programs. A year earlier she had met with a delegation of household workers. Because her own mother had worked as a domestic,

Shirley had a special understanding of their problems. In the New York State Assembly, she had succeeded in getting legislation passed that gave such workers unemployment insurance. At their first meeting in Washington, D.C., she had told the women how to organize themselves into a representative group. With an official name and elected officers, they could effectively request, or lobby for, legislation, and expect to be treated with respect. The women followed her instructions and returned to Washington in 1973, organized and ready to push their demands for a minimum wage.

In the 1973 session, she shepherded a bill through the House that increased the minimum wage and extended it to domestic workers. Shirley's persistence in gaining support for the measure led her to call Governor George C. Wallace, who had influence with many congressmen. As a result of that call, several Southern legislators voted for the bill. With the help of other members of Congress, she enlisted labor union support. The bill had enough votes to pass both the House and the Senate, but President Nixon would not sign it. Without the two-thirds majority needed to override his veto, the Minimum Wage Bill did not become law.

Chisholm and her staff were successful in saving the Office of Equal Opportunity (OEO) from Republican plans to dissolve it during the 1973 session. Responsible for many anti-poverty programs, the agency had helped poor people in the nation's cities to help themselves. Still learning how to develop effective programs, OEO made mistakes and was criticized for wasting money. Shirley knew that, like many experiments, the agency was imperfect. But she believed in correcting its mistakes instead of abandoning it. She convinced other members of Congress to resist the president's efforts to do away with OEO. But they were unable to fight administrative cuts that made the agency less effective.

Shirley Chisholm had another problem to face in 1973. Her presidential campaign had never raised all the money she needed and she had a large debt to repay. Even with fund-raisers, the burden of repayment fell almost completely on her. To pay the bills, she planned a full schedule of speaking engagements.

Then in September a report from the General Accounting Office (GAO) complicated her money problems. One of the functions of the federal agency was to screen political campaign expenditures. The GAO turned over its information about Chisholm campaign funds to the Justice Department for investigation. The agency cited four possible violations. Newspapers that reported the story mentioned the Chisholms' new house in the Virgin Islands and Shirley's fashionable clothes, but they failed to add that Shirley and Conrad could easily afford the house with their own money. The implication of misuse of funds was clear.

Shirley and Conrad knew the truth. Conrad had acted as principal advisor and unpaid aide. Unaware of all the federal election laws, he and the other non-professional campaign workers failed to disclose expenditures and keep adequate financial records. When several small corporate donations were declared illegal, they did not return the money immediately. Moreover, Conrad's name had not appeared on campaign stationery, as required. Inexperienced, and with so many demands on their time, the Chisholm campaign workers had made mistakes. When Shirley and Conrad discovered the errors, they corrected them.

Chisholm's outspoken protest against the war in Vietnam and other Nixon policies had made her unpopular with the administration. The choice of investigating *her* campaign, with its small amount of funding, seemed odd. Wise to the ways of Washington, Shirley branded the inquiry "a fishing expedition." Asked about the charges on her lecture tours, she patiently explained that if errors occurred, they were not deliberate. As she predicted, the tempest blew over. In April 1974, the Justice Department declared the case closed. It found no evidence of misconduct in handling campaign funds.

In February 1977, Shirley St. Hill Chisholm surprised the

public again when she and Conrad Chisholm were divorced. Differences had developed between them, not all related to the stress of politics. Drifting apart for a long time, they agreed to end their almost thirty-year marriage. Though no longer husband and wife, they have remained good friends.

Later that same year, Shirley married Arthur Hardwick, Jr. She had first met the handsome, exuberant widower ten years earlier, when they were both in the New York State Assembly. The first black assemblyman from upstate New York, Hardwick was a businessman who made his home in Buffalo. Although she maintained her Brooklyn address and continued to represent the Twelfth Congressional District, Shirley Chisholm Hardwick now also had a home in Buffalo, New York.

Shirley was reelected to the House of Representatives in every two-year term between 1974 and 1980. By then, she had earned seniority in the system that she had once scorned. She had become an effective congresswoman, capable of gaining support for important legislation. She had worked with other members of Congress to weld a strong liberal coalition in the House of Representatives.

In those years, however, the federal debt had soared and consumer prices were rising. The high cost of poverty programs was blamed for the inflation.

In 1978 and 1980, liberal senators and representatives were defeated by more conservative candidates who wanted to reduce federal spending. In the next few years, Shirley saw the break-up of the liberal coalition. Liberals who remained in Congress believed that they would have to tone down their own support for social programs in order to keep their seats. They also knew that President Ronald Reagan would veto bills for funding new programs.

Although she returned to Congress after the 1980 election, her heart wasn't in it. A year earlier, her second husband, Arthur Hardwick, Jr., had almost died in an automobile accident. Shirley was in Washington when the accident occurred. During his

Shirley Chisholm stands third to the left of President Gerald R. Ford as he signs a proclamation making August 26 Women's Equality Day, August 22, 1974.

recovery, she had to leave him regularly to attend to her congressional duties.

Her husband's accident and the new conservative climate in Washington prompted Shirley to think about her own goals. She had never intended staying in Congress for the rest of her life. Perhaps she could be as effective somewhere else.

One possibility was teaching. She had always felt a strong connection with the young. And even in her political career, she'd held on to the thread of teaching. She had tutored volunteers in the voter registration drives. During her own campaigns she had taught supporters how to organize. The domestic workers who came to Congresswoman Chisholm for help received lessons in how to get what they needed.

Then, in May 1981, Shirley was invited by Mount Holyoke College to deliver the commencement address and receive an honorary degree. She had spoken at many graduations and received numerous other honorary degrees. But this particular ceremony seemed special. Surveying the young women seated in the grassy amphitheater, she told them, "Ask questions and demand answers. Do not just tend your garden, collect your paycheck, bolt the door, and deplore what you see on television. Too many Americans are doing that already. Instead, you must live in the mainstream of your time and of your generation."

At the commencement weekend activities Shirley learned more about Mount Holyoke, and she liked what she learned. It was the oldest women's college in the country, and its president was a woman. At lunch with Dr. Joseph Ellis, the dean of faculty, she mentioned her thoughts about leaving Congress. Dr. Ellis told her that if she did, he hoped that she would join the Mount Holyoke faculty. He repeated the invitation in a letter, and after another visit to the campus, Shirley was ready to accept.

On February 10, 1982, Congresswoman Shirley Chisholm

called a press conference in her Washington office. The formal announcement of her retirement followed months of hints.

"I'm hanging up my hat," she said in an interview later. "I'm not going to lie. Many of us can't be effective at this time. Years ago I could effect alliances," she said. "But the 1980 defeat of liberal senators and representatives have changed all that. The coalitions are no longer there."

Shirley assured the poor and the powerless that she would continue as their spokesperson.

"My voice will be heard, but not as an elected official," she said. "I want people to know that this is not a funeral, politically."

Wesley McDonald Holder, Shirley's old political teacher and adviser, was angry and disappointed. The Twelfth Congressional District had other candidates, but they would never have another Shirley Chisholm. Shirley understood that she was giving up the seniority that she'd earned in Congress. She was the only woman on the powerful House Rules Committee and one of the longest-serving members of the Congressional Black Caucus. Her successor would have to start where she had begun fourteen years before, a freshman member of the House of Representatives. Shirley knew that Mac hated to end their close political association of more than twenty-five years.

But she had other plans. After many emotional farewells, Congresswoman Chisholm became Professor Chisholm. In taking leave of Washington, Shirley made it clear that she was not deserting the civil rights struggle or retiring from public life. "I won't be home at night knitting afghans," she said, as she left for South Hadley, Massachusetts, where the quiet Mount Holyoke campus was located.

In accepting the Mount Holyoke offer, Shirley Chisholm had been named Purington Professor, an appointed position filled earlier by other distinguished Americans. She would teach three days a week for eight months of the year. Purington Professors taught in the area of their expertise. Shirley's background had prepared her for teaching in several departments. She could have given a course in women's studies, black studies, Afro-American studies, or political science. Professor Richard Moran was eager to have her in the department of sociology and anthropology, where he was chairman.

Shirley Chisholm arrived at Mount Holyoke in time for the spring 1983 semester. She moved into a small, white, colonial-style house in South Hadley, at the edge of the campus. On Mondays, Tuesdays, and Wednesdays, she taught one course in politics and another on the social roles of women. In the small women's college, Shirley Chisholm was soon as at home as she had been in the halls of Congress and the streets of Brooklyn.

Younger colleagues loved to see her stride quickly up the hill on her way to classes, a stylish black cape flaring out behind her in the frosty New England air. They were astonished by her energy at an 8:00 A.M. class on Monday after flying in from a weekend of speaking engagements in Denver, Colorado, or some other faraway place. Her practical knowledge of government and politics stimulated both students and faculty. Although she was a celebrity and still received calls and requests for interviews, she never asked for any kind of special treatment. Shirley enjoyed the regular contact with students.

"I want to make my students think," she said. "I want them to participate, to ask questions. They can disagree with me on anything, but I warn them to back up their arguments."

The small college brought teachers and students together informally after classes. Shirley was in even more demand than other faculty members. She gladly accepted invitations to dormitory dinners, remembering how she had enjoyed after-class discussions with her Brooklyn College professors. Long after the dinner dishes were cleared, she went on answering questions and telling stories of her years in politics. Shirley's sense of humor brightened the accounts, but her intent was serious. She wanted these young

Shirley Chisholm, Purington Professor at Mount Holyoke College, 1985.

students to know the realities of government and politics and to think of becoming involved themselves.

Shirley's schedule was more flexible at the college than it had been in Congress. She was on campus at least three days a week and often four, but was then free to continue her busy speaking schedule. In the 1984 Democratic Party primary campaigns, she worked for Jesse Jackson's Democratic Party nomination. But she still had time to spend with her husband at the beautiful home he had built for them in Williamsville, outside Buffalo.

In 1985 she took a leave from Mount Holyoke to teach in the Scholars-in-Residence program at Spelman College, the black women's college in Atlanta, Georgia. In addition to her course, entitled, "Congress, Power, Politics, Policy," she met regularly with students in informal gatherings. That spring Spelman College dedicated the Shirley Chisholm Lounge.

Returning to Mount Holyoke from her leave, Shirley again shifted direction and closed the classroom door at the end of the spring semester in 1987. Her parting words to students reflected perennial Chisholm optimism.

"Pay absolutely no attention to doomsday criers around you," she told them. "Do your thing, whatever that may be, looking only to God, whomever your God is, and to your conscience for approval. That's how I did it."

Mount Holyoke was sorry to see Professor Chisholm leave. She had become a vital part of campus life. Saying good-bye, college president Elizabeth T. Kennen commented, "We wish, of course, that she could be here forever. I'm not sure we will ever fill the void Shirley Chisholm has left behind."

Arthur Hardwick, ill with cancer, had died in 1986. At his funeral in the Baptist church in Buffalo, old friends gathered to mourn with her. The large group went to the gravesite and then returned in vans to a luncheon at the church. The tables in the church hall that day, said Joseph Ellis of Mount Holyoke, "represented the last thirty years of American civil rights history and American political history."

The house in Williamsville was empty without Arthur Hardwick. But Shirley spent little time there. Another presidential year was approaching and the Reverend Jesse Jackson, for whom she had campaigned in the 1984 Democratic Party primaries, again needed her help. With Ronald Reagan's second term in the White House ending, the Democrats had a real chance to win back the presidency. The field was crowded, but Jesse Jackson's supporters had done their homework and were ready for an exciting campaign. To help broaden his base of support, Shirley Chisholm campaigned for Jackson in Hispanic and rural white areas.

Jackson took the country by storm in 1988. He demonstrated what Shirley Chisholm had pointed out fourteen years earlier in her presidential campaign: once united, blacks would wield powerful voting power. Jackson drew support from many segments of American society. Other minorities and working-class whites were proud to unite under the banner of Jackson's Rainbow Coalition.

Jesse Jackson's bid for the presidential nomination evoked memories of the 1972 Chisholm campaign. His New Jersey chairman, Newark Mayor Sharpe James, credited Shirley for paving the way. "If there had been no Shirley Chisholm, there would have been no 'Run, Jesse, run,' in 1984 and no 'Win, Jesse, win' in 1988," said James.

The 1988 Jackson campaign, like Chisholm's, went all the way to the Democratic National Convention. Interviewed outside the convention center in Atlanta in July 1988, Shirley expressed her disappointment with the party's vice-presidential choice. "The Democratic Party has two wings, the conservative and the moderate," she said. "And Jesse Jackson should have been offered the second spot because his followers represent that moderate wing. The party's going to have to learn that black people are not going to roll over and play dead anymore."

Shirley Chisholm, walking with her husband, Arthur Hardwick, prior to the Shirley Chisholm Lounge dedication ceremony, March 21, 1985.

Shirley Chisholm went to the convention, not as a delegate as in other years, but as head of the National Political Congress of Black Women (NPCBW). The group was organized after the 1984 Democratic national Convention. The 1984 Democratic presidential candidate, Walter Mondale, had considered a number of white males, black males, and white females to run for vice-president, but no black female. Earlier in 1984, Shirley had predicted that the vice-presidential spot would go to either a black or a female. With typical Chisholm humor, she remarked, "I meet both criteria—a twofer!" But Shirley could also think of several other black women who should be considered for the spot. When none of them was approached and when minority planks were lost in the platform, Shirley was determined to take action.

After the convention she gathered together nine black women in Washington, D.C. From that beginning came an historic, four-day meeting of five hundred black women at Spelman College in Atlanta, Georgia. They drew up a constitution and mission and chose Shirley Chisholm as leader. She and other black women in politics set out to build an organization that could not be ignored.

The NPCBW grew rapidly, with 8,500 members and chapters in 36 states by 1988. Both major parties now consult the NPCBW about election issues. The group sent a delegation of 100 women to the 1988 Democratic National Convention to present demands for promoting civil rights and social programs.

Shirley is enthusiastic about the NPCBW. Local chapters endorse and support candidates. An important outreach for Shirley Chisholm, the teacher, is its preparation of young women to enter the political process when they reach the voting age of 18. She wants them to learn early of the leadership opportunities in politics—opportunities that she, in large measure, made possible. Her time was passing, she realized, and she wanted the vacuum filled with young black women. She felt an obligation to pass on to the new generation all that she had learned.

Her message to young people was perhaps best expressed in her commencement address to the 1982 Spelman College graduates, when she accepted an honorary doctoral degree. "You are judged, and you are loved, for your personal qualities, your values, and your accomplishments. I know, from my own experience and from studying the lives of others, that success comes from doing, to the best of your ability, what you know in your heart are the *right* things to do."

Chisholm makes it a point to express her optimism, knowing that self-pity never accomplished anything. "I try to show that by the way that I behave. I'm always so open, so friendly, always so enthusiastic even though things look dark."

Still aware of her role as a leader, she promised, "I cannot afford to transfer to my own people who have been so disillusioned and downtrodden the fact that one of their own leaders feels the way they do." She believed, with the Reverend Jesse Jackson, that she had to offer hope.

But it is not as a politician that Shirley Chisholm would like to be remembered.

"I do not want to be remembered as the first black woman to be elected to the United States Congress, even though I am. I do not want to be remembered as the first woman who happened to be black to make a serious bid for the presidency. I'd like to be known as a catalyst for change, a woman who had the determination and a woman who had the perseverance to fight on behalf of the female population and the black population, because I'm a product of both, being black and a woman."

Chronology

1924 — November 30, in Brooklyn, New York, born Shirley Anita St. Hill, the first of four daughters to Charles and Ruby (Seale) St. Hill.

1946 — B.A., Brooklyn College, *cum laude*.

Began teaching at Mt. Calvary Day Care Center.

1949 — Married Conrad Chisholm. Marriage ended in divorce, 1977.

1951 — M.A., Early Childhood Education, Teachers College, Columbia University.

1959 — Appointed educational consultant, Division of Day Care, City of New York.

1964 — Elected to New York State Assembly. Served 1964-68.

1968 — Named National Democratic Party Committeewoman from New York.

Elected to the United States Congress. Reelected and served until 1980.

1972 — Ran for the Democratic Presidential nomination.

1977 — Married Arthur Hardwick, Jr., and moved to Williamsville, New York.

1982 — Retired from the United States Congress.

1983 — Appointed Purington Professor at Mount Holyoke College, South Hadley, Mass.

1985 — Appointed Scholar-in-Residence at Spelman College, Atlanta, Ga.

1985 — National Political Congress of Black Women organized, with Chisholm as first president.

1988 — Campaigned for Jesse Jackson for Democratic Party presidential nomination.

Index